World
History Series

Women of Ancient Greece

Titles in the World History Series

Series ■■■

Women of
Ancient Greece

by
Don Nardo

Lucent Book   o, CA 92198-9011

On Cover: *The Garden of the Hesperids, red figure vase painting, fourth century* B.C.

Library of Congress Cataloging-in-Publication Data

Nardo, Don, 1947–
    Women of Ancient Greece / Don Nardo.
       p.   cm.—(World history series)
    Includes bibliographical references and index.
    Summary: Describes women in ancient Greece through the Hellenistic age, including their legal rights and status, their home life, their roles in community activities, and their image in mythology, drama, and philosophy.
    ISBN 1-56006-646-6 (lib. : alk. paper)

    1. Women—Greece—History—Juvenile literature. 2. Women—History—To 500—Juvenile literature. 3. Greece—Citizen—To 146 B.C.—Juvenile literature. [1. Women—Greece—History. 2. Women—History—To 500. 3. Greece—Civilization—To 146 B.C.] I. Title. II. Series.
HQ1134.N37 2000
305.4'0938—dc21
                                  99-053699
                                        CIP

Contents

Foreword

Each year on the first day of school, nearly every history teacher faces the task of explaining why his or her students should study history. One logical answer to this question is that exploring what happened in our past explains how the things we often take for granted—our customs, ideas, and institutions—came to be. As statesman and historian Winston Churchill put it, "Every nation or group of nations has its own tale to tell. Knowledge of the trials and struggles is necessary to all who would comprehend the problems, perils, challenges, and opportunities which confront us today." Thus, a study of history puts modern ideas and institutions in perspective. For example, though the founders of the United States were talented and creative thinkers, they clearly did not invent the concept of democracy. Instead, they adapted some democratic ideas that had originated in ancient Greece and with which the Romans, the British, and others had experimented. An exploration of these cultures, then, reveals their very real connection to us through institutions that continue to shape our daily lives.

Another reason often given for studying history is the idea that lessons exist in the past from which contemporary societies can benefit and learn. This idea, although controversial, has always been an intriguing one for historians. Those who agree that society can benefit from the past often quote philosopher George Santayana's famous statement, "Those who cannot remember the past are condemned to repeat it." Historians who subscribe to Santayana's philosophy believe that, for example, studying the events that led up to the major world wars or other significant historical events would allow society to chart a different and more favorable course in the future.

Just as difficult as convincing students to realize the importance of studying history is the search for useful and interesting supplementary materials that present historical events in a context that can be easily understood. The volumes in Lucent Books' World History Series attempt to present a broad, balanced, and penetrating view of the march of history. Ancient Egypt's important wars and rulers, for example, are presented against the rich and colorful backdrop of Egyptian religious, social, and cultural developments. The series engages the reader by enhancing historical events with these cultural contexts. For example, in Ancient Greece, the text covers the role of women in that society. Slavery is discussed in The Roman Empire, as well as how slaves earned their freedom. The numerous and varied aspects of everyday life in these and other societies are explored in each volume of the series. Additionally, the series covers the major political, cultural, and philosophical ideas as the torch of civilization is passed from ancient Mesopotamia and Egypt, through Greece, Rome, Medieval Europe, and other world cultures, to the modern day.

The material in the series is formatted in a thorough, precise, and organized manner. Each volume offers the reader a comprehensive and clearly written overview of an important historical event or period. The topic under discussion is placed in a broad, historical context. For example, The Italian Renaissance begins with a discussion of the High Middle Ages and the loss of central control that allowed certain Italian cities to develop artistically. The book ends by looking forward to the Reformation and interpreting the societal changes that grew out of the Renaissance. Thus, students are not only involved in an historical era, but also enveloped by the events leading up to that era and the events following it.

One important and unique feature in the World History Series is the primary and secondary source quotations that richly supplement each volume. These quotes are useful in a number of ways. First, they allow students access to sources they would not normally be exposed to because of the difficulty and obscurity of the original source. The quotations range from interesting anecdotes to farsighted cultural perspectives and are drawn from historical witnesses both past and present. Second, the quotes demonstrate how and where historians themselves derive their information on the past as they strive to reach a consensus on historical events. Lastly, all of the quotes are footnoted, familiarizing students with the citation process and allowing them to verify quotes and/or look up the original source if the quote piques their interest.

Finally, the books in the World History Series provide a detailed launching point for further research. Each book contains a bibliography specifically geared toward student research. A second, annotated bibliography introduces students to all the sources the author consulted when compiling the book. A chronology of important dates gives students an overview, at a glance, of the topic covered. Where applicable, a glossary of terms is included.

In short, the series is designed not only to acquaint readers with the basics of history, but also to make them aware that their lives are a part of an ongoing human saga. Perhaps they will then come to the same realization as famed historian Arnold Toynbee. In his monumental work, A Study of History, he wrote about becoming aware of history flowing through him in a mighty current, and of his own life "welling like a wave in the flow of this vast tide."

A Limited but Tantalizing Picture of Greek Women

In reading this volume, those who were formerly unfamiliar with ancient Greek society will be immediately struck, probably surprised, and perhaps disturbed at most Greek men's treatment of Greek women as inferiors. Indeed, throughout antiquity most Greek women had few or no civil rights and many enjoyed little freedom of choice or social mobility. Moreover, nearly everyone, including most women, accepted this state of affairs as the natural way of things. By contrast, to modern eyes it appears decidedly unnatural, unjust, and unworthy of a society that was in many other ways unusually advanced and enlightened for its time.

Yet before condemning ancient Greek men as insensitive and inhumane, we must first consider the unique vantage from which we look back on the past. Most people in the United States and other modern industrialized nations tend to take for granted certain social and ethical notions, among them the worth and dignity of all human beings, including women. Most of these countries have laws that grant equal rights to women; and a majority of girls in these societies are routinely raised and socialized to believe that they are every bit as capable as boys and deserving of the same opportunities.

What makes this idea of female equality so unique is that it is a very recent development. Throughout most of history,

This bust of a Greek woman now rests in the National Archaeological Museum in Athens. The eyes and hair were originally painted to appear more lifelike.

among almost all societies, races, and religions, women were seen as naturally inferior and subservient to men. All ancient societies, that of Greece among them, treated women as inferior, for instance. Male-dominated medieval European societies did the same, often citing passages in the Bible or writings by noted religious figures like Saint Paul or Saint Augustine to support the notion that God made men in his own image and created women to serve and obey men. The occasional strong and accomplished women—Spain's Queen Isabella, France's Joan of Arc, and England's Queen Elizabeth I, for example—were viewed as impressive but "unnatural" exceptions to the rule.

Not until the 1600s and 1700s, when a few enlightened philosophers suggested that women might be as worthy as men, did this view begin to change. And even then, actual political and social reforms were extremely slow in coming. For instance, Australia did not grant women the right to vote until 1902, Britain not until 1918, the United States not until 1920, and the modern nation of Greece not until 1951. Regarding women's status and treatment, therefore, it is the modern developed world, rather than ancient Greece, that is (fortunately for women) unusual and out of step with the trends of history.

It would be a mistake, however, to generalize about the lives of ancient Greek women. Though nearly always regarded as less worthy than men, their status, treatment, and opportunities were far from the same in all Greek cities, states, and realms and at all times. Modern scholars divide ancient Greek history into several broad eras: the Bronze Age (ca. 3000–ca. 1100 B.C.); Dark Age (ca. 1100–ca. 800 B.C.); Archaic Age (ca. 800–ca. 500 B.C.); Classic Age (ca. 500–323 B.C.); and Hellenistic Age (323–30 B.C.). Women's legal status, social mobility, and economic opportunities differed by varying degrees from one age to another. And women in Athens apparently led markedly more restricted, regulated lives and had fewer opportunities for self-expression than women in some other Greek states. For example, in Sparta (located in the southern part of the Peloponnesus, the large peninsula that composes the southern third of Greece), women could take part in athletic training and own land at the same time that Athenian women were denied these privileges.

Our picture of ancient Greek women is further complicated and also limited by the fact that the bulk of the surviving evidence about them comes from Athens. (A fair amount is known about Spartan social customs and women, but very little information about these aspects of other Greek states has survived.) Because Athens was long the largest and one of the most influential Greek city-states, many early modern scholars felt safe in using its social customs as models for Greek social customs in general. According to this view, the lives of women in most Greek states were very similar to those of Athenian women; and Spartan customs, including those pertaining to women, were atypical, exceptional, and/or odd.

However, later scholarship cast doubt on this scenario. And most experts now feel that, while Sparta was unusually liberal and equable in its treatment of women,

Athens was unusually conservative and restrictive. Therefore, most Greek states fell somewhere in between, most of them granting more freedom and opportunities to women than Athens did. Other changing views of Greek women are part of an ongoing renaissance in the study of ancient Greek families, private life, social and sexual roles, and other aspects of social history that were long neglected by historians in favor of political and military history. The first major, in-depth study of ancient Greek women was Sarah B. Pomeroy's *Goddesses, Whores, Wives, and Slaves: Women in Classical Antiquity*, published in 1975. Several excellent volumes appeared in the 1980s and 1990s, including one by Pomeroy on Greek women in the Hellenistic Age (1984) and a thoughtful general study by University of London scholar Sue Blundell (1995); and new books and articles on the subject appear each year.

It must be emphasized, however, that the picture of Greek women painted in these studies, including that of Athenian women, remains to a large degree unclear and speculative. This is because of the nature of the evidence, particularly the written sources. Not only have few non-Athenian sources survived, but the vast majority of those that have were not written by women and therefore do not constitute direct testimony. As Pomeroy herself states in the introduction to her groundbreaking 1975 book,

> The literary testimony presents grave problems for the social historian. Women pervade nearly every genre of classical [ancient Greek and Roman] literature, yet often the bias of the author distorts the information. Aside from some scraps of lyric poetry, the extant [surviving] formal literature of classical antiquity was all

Six caryatids—pillars carved in the shape of women—hold up the roof of the famed Porch of the Maidens, on the south façade of the Erechtheum, one of the temples of Athena on the Athenian Acropolis.

written by men. In addition, misogyny [dislike of women] taints much ancient literature [since most men, including the writers, believed women were fundamentally inferior to men].[1]

Thus, scholars must be very careful and critical in examining the ancient written sources available to them about Greek women. Besides the handful of women's poems and fragments of poems that Pomeroy mentions, those sources include the works of male poets, from Homer and Hesiod in the Archaic Age to Theocritus in Hellenistic times; the plays of Euripides and other great fifth-century B.C. dramatists; the essays of philosophers, most notably Plato and Aristotle (both fourth century B.C.), who discuss women's natural and/or ideal social status; writings from the Greek medical school founded by the noted fifth-century B.C. physician Hippocrates, which deal with female anatomy and common female medical conditions; the works of a few late Greek historians and biographers, most notably Plutarch (first century A.D.), who recorded anecdotes about the personalities and activities of certain women; and the speeches of orators (mostly fourth-century B.C. Athenians), especially those written for court litigants, which reveal various aspects of women's private lives and legal status.

These formal written sources are supplemented by various kinds of archaeological evidence. These include depictions of women in sculpture, vase and wall paintings, mosaics, and on coins; tombstone epitaphs and other inscriptions; graffiti on the walls of buildings; personal artifacts, such as jewelry, grooming items, looms, and so on; and scraps of papyrus (a kind of paper), containing fragments of letters, prayers, and marriage contracts and other legal documents pertaining to women (mostly from Hellenistic Egypt). Though meager, these pieces of evidence afford us a tantalizing glimpse into the lives of a remarkable people long dead and a gender sadly long oppressed.

Chapter

1 Women in Early Greek Societies

Concrete evidence for the lives of the earliest Greek women is so meager that any full, clear picture of their labors, loves, words, hopes, and dreams was long ago lost in the mists of time. Not only does most of the ancient evidence about Greek women come from Athens, but the vast majority of it is from the Classic and Hellenistic Ages (together encompassing the fifth through first centuries B.C.). Little is known about either the historical or social aspects of the Bronze, Dark, and Archaic Ages; what *is* known has been pieced together painstakingly from some widely scattered archaeological evidence, a few surviving pieces of early literature, and the characters and stories in Greek myths.

It must be emphasized that literature and myths are not straightforward history. So the manner in which women are portrayed in such sources is not as accurate and reliable as depictions of the lives of real women. Still, the stories told in the early literature and myths are set most often in the real world. And modern scholars believe that they contain various elements that reflect some of the basic social realities of the time.

This figurine, found at Tanagra in central Greece, shows a young woman draped from head to foot in a folded garment called a himation.

THE HOMERIC EPICS

The most famous and important of these early literary-mythological sources are the epic poems of Homer, a semilegendary Greek poet who may have lived in the eighth century B.C. The more than fifteen thousand-line *Iliad* describes an episode in the last year of the ten-year siege of the fortified city of Troy (on the northwestern coast of Asia Minor, what is now Turkey) by a coalition of Greek kings. And the twelve thousand-line *Odyssey* tells of the wanderings of one of these rulers, Odysseus (king of the island kingdom of Ithaca), in the years following Troy's fall. From at least the early sixth century B.C. on, the Greeks viewed these works as vital sources of literary, artistic, moral, social, educational, and political instruction as well as practical wisdom. They also served as a culturally unifying force, the common property of all Greeks, emphasizing their shared cultural identity.

Putting aside the importance of the Homeric poems to the classical Greeks, what can these works tell us about the Greeks of earlier eras? Do they describe some aspects of real society, and if so, which society—that of the Bronze Age or the Dark Age? First, there may or may not have been a real, historical Greek siege of Troy. If there was, it likely occurred between about 1250 and 1200 B.C., for excavators have found evidence that the city was besieged and sacked sometime in that interval. If the attackers were in fact Greek, they were Mycenaeans, the name given by modern scholars

This painting from the Renaissance depicts a scene from Homer's Odyssey *in which Odysseus's wife, Penelope, works her loom while her suitors look on.*

to the inhabitants of the fortress-palaces and kingdoms of Greece in the late Bronze Age. Even if the Mycenaeans did besiege Troy, the specific characters and events in Homer's epics are at least highly exaggerated and romanticized, if not wholly fictional. Yet that does not necessarily lessen their value as windows into early Greek society. "For our purposes [i.e., the study of early Greek women]," writes University of Parma scholar Eva Cantarella,

> the question [of the Trojan War's historical reality] is irrelevant—the poems do not interest [us] as a record of events, but as a document that transmits the memory of a culture. . . . Even if the situations described are not true, they must be realistic. The characters surely behave according to the rules of real society; the ethic that inspired their deeds must be that which the poetry . . . taught and transmitted. The society described in the *Iliad* and the *Odyssey* is, in other words, a mirror of Greek society.[2]

The consensus of scholarly opinion is that Homer kept alive a dim memory of Bronze Age kings and heroes and their royal courts and exploits; but that he transplanted them into the real social setting of his own time—the late Dark Age and early Archaic Age.

EARLY EXAMPLES OF MISOGYNY

The Homeric poems should, therefore, provide at least a partial glimpse into women's lives in Dark Age Greece and perhaps to a lesser extent in Bronze Age Greece as well. One of the first impressions one gets is that Homeric women (excluding the fanciful goddesses and sorceresses) are on the whole subservient to men. Also, for the most part the women are expected to attend to domestic matters, such as rearing children and running the home, and are often regarded with suspicion by the men. Misogyny, which can manifest itself as men's mistrust as well as their dislike of women, was apparently already well established in this era.

Some of the religious myths that emerged during the Dark Age also depict women as inferior in worth and not to be trusted. The most obvious example is the story of Pandora, the first woman, as told by the poet

A Renaissance depiction of a famous woman from Greek mythology, Pandora, the first woman, who inadvertently let loose the ills of the world.

Hesiod, who flourished about 700 B.C., in the generation following Homer. According to Hesiod, Zeus, the leader of the Greek gods, wanted to punish Prometheus (one of the Titans, an earlier race of gods) for teaching humans how to use fire. At Zeus's order Hephaestos, the god of the forge, fashioned Pandora from clay and various gods endowed her with physical and mental gifts (hence her name, meaning "all gifts"). The chief god then sent the maiden to Epimetheus, Prometheus's slow-witted brother. Prometheus had warned his brother not to accept any gifts from the gods, but Epimetheus took Pandora in anyway, after which she proceeded, unwittingly, to open a jar and unleash all the evils that thereafter plagued the human race. By venting his wrath on the humans, Prometheus's cherished creations, Zeus had managed indirectly to punish the disobedient Titan.

The openly misogynistic Hesiod called Pandora "the hopeless trap, deadly to men." From her, he says in his poem the *Theogony*, "comes all the race of womankind, the deadly female race and tribe of wives who live with mortal men and bring them harm, no help to them in poverty but ready enough to share with them in wealth."[3] One of Hesiod's younger contemporaries, the poet Semonides, agreed, writing, "This is the worst plague Zeus has made—women. . . . The man who lives with a woman never goes through all his day in cheerfulness. . . . Each man will take care to praise his own wife and find fault with the other's; we do not realize that the fate of all of us [men] is alike."[4]

Certain assumptions can probably safely be made from these poets' descriptions of women. Both men were likely nonaristocrats; Hesiod, for instance, the son of a maritime trader who became a farmer, describes his own struggles to scratch a living from the soil in his *Works and Days*. This suggests that his wife and the other women of which he speaks were of average means and were therefore fairly representative of average Greek women of his day. Also, his and Semonides' negative remarks about women are consistent with a strongly patriarchal society where it was acceptable for men to insult women openly; and as studies of modern families and households show, verbal abuse of women often escalates to the physical variety. Yet that does not necessarily mean that most early Greek wives were simpering, battered creatures who, out of fear, remained silent and could not express their opinions. In fact, both Hesiod and Semonides frequently refer to women who are strong-willed, demanding, nagging, opinionated, assertive, and vindictive; and apparently the fact that their wives and other women often did not "know their place" was a major factor contributing to the poets' overall negative view of women.

SOME STRONG, RESOURCEFUL WOMEN

Did Hesiod's and Semonides' harsh descriptions and open contempt of womankind represent the view of most men of their time? Or were these writers just scarred and bitter over some bad personal experiences with their own wives, sisters, and/or other women? Unfortunately,

Women as Sows, Bitches, and Monkeys

The sixth-century B.C. male poet Semonides may have written his poem On Women *(excerpted here from Lefkowitz's and Fant's sourcebook) as a sort of social satire in the manner of Aesop's fables. But though its style is exaggerated and meant to be humorous, Semonides' contempt and mistrust of women come through loud and clear.*

"In the beginning the god made the female mind separately [i.e., made different kinds of women]. One he made from a long-bristled sow. In her house everything lies in disorder, smeared with mud . . . and she herself unwashed, in clothes unlaundered, sits by the dungheap and grows fat. Another he made from a wicked vixen; a woman who [thinks she] knows everything. . . . She often calls a good thing bad and a bad thing good. Her attitude is never the same. Another he made from a bitch. . . . She peers everywhere and strays everywhere, always yapping, even if she sees no human being. A man cannot stop her by threatening, nor by losing his temper and knocking out her teeth . . . but [she] ceaselessly keeps up a barking you can do nothing with. . . . Another he made from the sea; she has two characters. One day she smiles and is happy. . . . But on another day she is unbearable to look at or come near to; then she raves so that you can't approach her, like a bitch over her pups. . . . Another is from a monkey. . . . Her face is hideous; when a woman like her goes through the town, everyone laughs at her. She is short in the neck; she moves awkwardly; she has no bottom and is all legs. Hard luck on the man who holds such a misery in his arms!"

given the lack of conclusive evidence, these questions cannot be answered for certain. However, it is instructive that both Hesiod and Semonides occasionally conceded that admirable women did exist. Describing the "good" kind of wife, Semonides says, "The man who gets her is fortunate, for . . . she causes his property to grow and increase, and she grows old with a husband whom she loves and

who loves her, the mother of a handsome and reputable family."[5]

Some positive views of women also appear in Homer's epics. Though the women in these works are generally subservient to men, they are by no means portrayed as incompetent or lowly. In the *Odyssey*, for example, Odysseus has enough confidence and trust in his wife, Penelope, to leave her in charge of his kingdom when he goes off to Troy. "I cannot say whether the gods will let me come back," he tells her, "or whether I shall fall on Trojan soil. But I leave everything here in your charge."[6] And in the *Iliad,* Agamemnon, the king of Mycenae and the leader of the expedition, leaves the care of his own kingdom in the hands of his wife, Clytemnestra. Granted, in such situations a male relative or court official usually kept an eye on and advised the queen in her husband's absence. Yet however much actual power she may have wielded, she was still the queen, a position of dignity and high respect. And in this position she, along with the wives of other prominent men, was often able to express her opinions no less forcefully than Hesiod's wife and other working-class women could.

Moreover, several of Homer's female characters have strong, vigorous personalities and enjoy marriages in which their husbands love and respect them. In the *Il-*iad, when the Trojan champion Hector prepares to leave the city and make a foray against the besieging Greeks, he first seeks out his wife, Andromache, who has been searching for him just as fervently. Their meeting at the Scaean Gate, which is one of the most touching and moving scenes in literature, depicts a relationship of mutual caring and tenderness. Though she knows her place is with her son (whom she holds in her arms) and that the fighting is "man's work," she does not hesitate to offer Hector her view of how to deploy his forces: "Draw your armies up where the wild fig tree stands, there where the city lies most open to assault, the walls [being] lower, [and more] easily overrun. Three times they [the Greeks] have tried that point, hoping to storm Troy."[7] Hector listens to her respectfully. Then he tells her how the mental image of his own brothers dying in battle is not nearly as painful to him as the thought of Andromache, after

This nineteenth-century etching shows Andromache bidding her husband, the Trojan hero Hector, farewell just prior to his fight to the death with Achilles. A nurse holding their infant son looks on.

his own death and Troy's fall, being dragged off as a slave to distant Greece. "No, no," he exclaims, "let the earth come piling over my dead body before I hear your cries, [before] I hear you dragged away!"[8]

The bond between Odysseus and Penelope in the *Odyssey* is also an extraordinarily strong and positive one. This is partly because Homer portrays the two characters as alike in many ways. During the twenty years they are apart, both are forced into situations in which they must and do employ considerable cunning and resourcefulness. They also display great perseverance, as each never stops longing that they will be reunited in their marriage bed (which he had built himself using a live olive tree as one bedpost). In the end that reunion takes place, and they are so overwhelmed with joy that they both shed tears. To prolong this touching scene for the lovers, Athena, the goddess of wisdom, delays the coming of dawn.

WHEN WOMEN WERE IN CHARGE?

Strong female characters like Andromache and Penelope were, in a sense, composites of the real women of Homer's day and the legendary queens and noblewomen of the Age of Heroes (the classical Greeks' name for what we call the late Bronze Age). On the one hand, these characters' personal attributes—loyalty, intelligence, resourcefulness, and so on—were probably modeled on similar qualities in Dark Age women. On the other hand,

their queenly images were likely dim memories from the Bronze Age, when kings ruled over formal royal courts and at least some queens and other noblewomen may have achieved positions of considerable power and influence.

We know, for example, that the Minoans (the Bronze Age inhabitants of the large Greek island of Crete) worshiped mostly female gods, the most important being Potnia ("the Lady"), who may have been an early manifestation of Athena. And the Minoan religion was dominated by priestesses who, some evidence suggests, were more powerful and revered than male priests. The degree to which such female authority extended into the political realm, if it did so at all, is unknown.

Over the years some scholars have suggested that women did indeed wield considerable political power in the Bronze Age and perhaps long before that period. In their view, Potnia and similar ancient goddesses worshiped by other Mediterranean and Near Eastern peoples were all manifestations of the Magna Mater, or "Great Mother." Supposedly, the existence of this all-powerful deity at the head of the early Bronze Age pantheon (group of gods) is evidence of a matriarchy (a society dominated by women and therefore the converse of a patriarchy).

Also frequently cited as evidence for an early matriarchy are Greek tales about the Amazons, a fabulous tribe of warrior women. Warfare between these women and Greek men (which the Greeks called Amazonomachy), became a common theme depicted in classical Greek literature, sculpture, and painting. (The location of the

Penelope Stands Up to the Suitors

In this excerpt from Homer's Odyssey *(E. V. Rieu's translation), Penelope, wife of Odysseus and queen of Ithaca, takes advantage of her high social status to display her personal courage and assertiveness. In the scene, she confronts and scolds the suitors who have been pressuring her to choose one of them as a husband (since they mistakenly assume that Odysseus, who did not return after Troy's fall, is dead).*

"It was at this moment that Penelope gave way to a sudden impulse to confront these suitors of hers, now that they had shown to what extremes they were prepared to go. She knew well enough that her son's [Telemachus's] murder had been canvassed [discussed] in the palace [by the suitors]. . . . So now . . . with queenly dignity she approached the young men . . . took her stand by a pillar . . . [and] rounded on Antinous [a leading suitor] and called him bluntly to account: 'They say in Ithaca that there is no one of your age so wise and eloquent as you, Antinous. You have proved them wrong; and I denounce you for the double-dealing ruffian that you are. Madman! How dare you plot against Telemachus's life and dishonor the obligations [you owe this house]? . . . Or have you forgotten that your father once sought refuge here from the fury of the mob. . . [that] would have killed him and had his heart out . . . had Odysseus not intervened and controlled their violence—Odysseus, at whose expense you are living free of charge, whose wife you are courting, and whose son you propose to kill. . . . I command you now to put an end of this and make the rest [of the suitors] obey you.'"

A nineteenth-century woodcut pictures Penelope staring out to sea, pining for her husband's return.

The Amazons were mythical warrior women who figured prominently in Greek art. This is a modern artist's rendition of Penthesilea, one of their fabled queens.

Amazons' homeland varied from one myth to another, but most often cited were the then-wild and little-known steppes lying west and north of the Black Sea.) The Amazons got their name from their supposed custom of cutting off one breast to allow for more effective use of bows, spears, and other weapons. The term *a-mazon* means "without breast." Their society was all-female and was therefore not a matriarchy in the strict sense since that would require a society that contained both men and women, with women dominating men. But some who argue that Greek society was originally matriarchal suggest that the Amazon myths are distorted, oversimplified memories of a time when women were indeed in charge.

There is no compelling evidence, however, for any such matriarchal Greek society. First, the Amazon myths were most popular in literature and art in Athens in the Classic Age, a place and time in which women were more regulated and restricted by men than in any other Greek city or era. This suggests that men manipulated and embellished these stories as negative role models to help legitimize their treatment of women. According to Sue Blundell,

> The message of the myths for both males and females alike was that in a civilized society women are passive, chaste, and married. The alternative—behaving like an Amazon—was a mark of barbarism, and its consequences were disastrous both for the women themselves and for the state over which they ruled. In this way the personal and political dominance of men was justified and reinforced.[9]

Greek men also exploited the Amazon myths for artistic reasons. In the Classic Age, particularly in Athens, it was considered unseemly to paint or sculpt nude or athletic women, at least Greek women; so by choosing the non-Greek, barbaric Amazons for his subjects, an artist could show young athletic women without appearing improper.

Likewise, the existence of high priestesses and even queens in the Bronze Age is insufficient evidence for a matriarchal society. First, it is unknown whether such socially prominent women possessed any significant political power. And even if they did, it was likely only on an intermittent and temporary basis, such as when a queen ruled after her husband's death,

This superb ancient stone statue of an Amazon warrior is likely a Roman copy of a Greek bronze original.

perhaps until her son was old enough to assume power. As Sarah B. Pomeroy aptly puts it, "No one would call Renaissance Britain a matriarchy because of the reigns of Mary Stuart, Mary Tudor, and Elizabeth [I]. Accordingly, the question of Bronze Age matriarchy remains the subject of tantalizing speculation."[10]

MINOAN VERSUS MYCENAEAN WOMEN

Even if Bronze Age Minoan women were not in charge, certain clues suggest that they enjoyed more freedom and respect than Greek women did in later eras. Archaeological evidence, including surviving art, shows that, in addition to the high status of women in the religious sphere, women took part in hunts; athletic events, including jumping over the backs of bulls; and in public ceremonies right alongside men. And women's quarters in the Minoan palaces were not separated and shut off from other areas, suggesting that there was no social segregation of women. It must be emphasized, however, that the women who lived in these palaces and were depicted in art were probably aristocrats or were at least upper-class ladies. Virtually nothing is known about lower-class Minoan women, who made up the bulk of the female population, except that some of them were slaves. It would be inappropriate, therefore, to draw general conclusions about Minoan women from the meager evidence at hand.

Similarly, it would be inaccurate to generalize about women in the Bronze Age solely from the Minoan evidence. The mainland Mycenaeans conquered and absorbed the island-centered Minoan sphere toward the end of the Bronze Age, and this later Mycenaean society differed in some significant ways from its predecessor. "First of all," Eva Cantarella explains,

> Mycenaean religion worshiped numerous male gods, such as Zeus, Poseidon, Ares, Hermes, and Dionysus, as well as female deities. . . . The architectural remains indicate that the areas of the [Mycenaean] palaces reserved for the women were more separate from the rest of the building complex [than in Minoan palaces]. . . . [Evidence also shows a breakdown of labor into] female and male tasks. The men (besides holding all positions of command) did the work of sheep rearing . . . and they managed the female labor groups. Women handled, stored, and distributed cereals . . . [and made] cloth. Hence, in the organization of [Mycenaean] female labor . . . we can identify certain characteristics of female labor that were to remain constant in later Greek society.[11]

Indeed, there seems to have been a rough continuity in the social status, roles, and duties of both men and women from the late Mycenaean era into the Dark Age that followed it. Men were political leaders, warriors, hunters, and traders; meanwhile, woman tended to the home, raised the children, cooked, and made clothes. This is certainly the way Homer depicts male-female social roles and division of labor, along with his dominating, sometimes misogynistic men and subservient, though often strong and admirable women.

How Women Lived in Archaic Times

There also seems to have been considerable continuity in the treatment of women during the transition from the Dark Age to the Archaic Age in the early eighth century B.C., the most widely accepted period for Homer's life. During Archaic times, the Greek world underwent a series of profound political, social, and economic changes. Among these were the expansion of local populations and a revival of trade and commerce, setting in motion the rapid colonization of the coasts of the Mediterranean and Black Seas; important agricultural developments, including more intensive cultivation of olives and vines and the rise of small independent farmers,

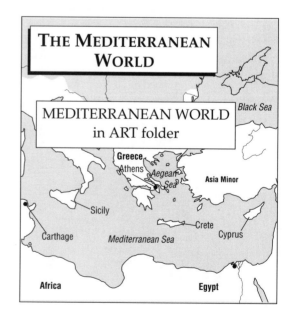

THE MEDITERRANEAN WORLD

MEDITERRANEAN WORLD in ART folder

Black Sea

Greece
Athens
Aegean Sea

Asia Minor

Sicily

Crete

Cyprus

Carthage

Mediterranean Sea

Africa

Egypt

This nineteenth-century woodcut depicts a group of well-to-do Greek women engaging in routine household duties while a domestic slave does some laundry nearby.

who became the economic backbone of individual communities; the development of isolated village communities into full-blown city-states (each city-state, or *polis*, made up of a central town and its surrounding villages and farmlands), each of which saw itself as a separate nation; the reappearance of reading and writing and the emergence of written literature (including Homer's epics and the poetry of Hesiod, Semonides, and others, including a few women); the development of monumental architecture, most conspicuously in religious temples; and widespread political experimentation, laying the groundwork for the emergence of democratic institutions in the Classic Age to come.

It is perhaps surprising that amid all of this complex and energetic activity and change the lives and roles of women ap-

pear to have altered very little. Society was still patriarchal, with the man the head of the household and lord or guardian *(kyrios)* of its women; society was also mainly patrilineal, meaning that the family name and property passed in inheritance from father to son; and the household, the abode of the basic social unit—the family *(oikos)*—was still the main focus of women's lives. Typical duties of free women included maintaining and rotating the household food storage, supervising the household slaves (in those families that could afford slaves; even well-to-do families appear to have had relatively few slaves in Archaic times), and either cooking or overseeing the slaves who cooked. Women also did all the spinning and weaving, laundered the clothes, bathed their husbands, and oversaw the dressing of corpses and other funeral preparations. In well-to-do households, female slaves performed most of the same duties, often working right alongside their mistresses; in some households, however, a slave woman might also be expected to have sex with the *kyrios* when he so desired (which must have led to friction and enmity among some wives and female slaves).

Not surprisingly, this male-controlled system put free women in a position of dependence, financially and otherwise, on their fathers, husbands, and sons. (That slave women were dependent on their masters is a given.) However, some women, apparently mainly poor ones, had jobs outside the home, either to supplement the family income or, as in the case of a widow with no grown sons, to support herself and her children. In the *Iliad*, Homer mentions "a working widow" who "holds the scales, painstakingly grips the beam and lifts the weight and the wool together, balancing both sides even, struggling to win a grim subsistence for her children"[12] (i.e., she earns her living by weighing wool on a scale). And in the *Works and Days*, Hesiod advises farmers to hire girls (preferably those without young children to distract them) to help out with chores. Women also worked as nursemaids, housekeepers, and mourners, singing laments at the funerals of well-to-do individuals. To work outside the home, women had to have a certain amount of freedom of movement and association. And evidence suggests that in the Archaic Age women, both poor and well-to-do, were not always confined in the home; although when they did go out to work or to visit family or friends, it was considered proper to wear a veil or to walk with a relative or family slave.

A WOMAN POET

This issue of female freedom of movement and association brings to mind the most famous Greek woman of Archaic times— Sappho. Born in the late seventh century B.C. on the island of Lesbos (off the coast of Asia Minor), she was one of the most revered poets of the ancient world. Most of her poems are lost, but the one complete poem and more than a hundred fragments of others that have survived provide some information about her life. For instance, in one fragment she reveals, "I have a beautiful daughter, golden like a flower, my beloved Cleis."[13] Like this one, most of the other fragments display her personal feelings and emotions with unusual directness, honesty, and sometimes decided intensity. Some also contain erotic qualities and references.

The main question that modern scholars continue to debate about Sappho is the nature of the audience for which she wrote. Clues in her poems suggest that she belonged to a group of female companions who gathered on a regular basis. Some scholars think the group was educational in nature, with younger women receiving instruction in poetry, music, and other subjects from a well-educated older woman, which may have been customary on Lesbos and in other Greek areas. In

IMMORTAL SAPPHO

These three fragments of Sappho's poems (Josephine Balmer's translation) are typical of her work. Fragment 2 expresses love in a powerful, highly personal way unmatched by most male Greek poets; Fragment 62 is part of a festive wedding song; and Fragment 106 is Sappho's recognition, perhaps the first such in Western literature, that an artist's work might bring him or her a kind of immortality.

2

"Love makes me tremble yet again, sapping all the strength from my limbs; bittersweet, undefeated creature—against you there is no defense."

62

"Lucky bridegroom, the marriage you have prayed for has come to pass and the bride you dreamed of is yours. . . . Beautiful bride, to look at you gives joy; your eyes are like honey, love flows over your gentle face. . . . Aphrodite [goddess of love] has honored you above all others."

106

"The Muses [goddesses who inspire artists] have made me happy in my lifetime and when I die I shall never be forgotten."

A bust of Sappho created centuries after her death. No one knows what she actually looked like.

that case, Sappho's poems would have been written and recited privately for a select few. By contrast, other scholars contend that the group was religious in nature, meeting to worship Aphrodite, the goddess of love, as well as the Muses and the Graces, the minor goddesses thought to endow humans with creativity and grace. In this scenario, Sappho's poems were written and performed publicly as part of the rituals attending these deities.

Whichever version is more accurate (or perhaps it was some combination of the two), the important point is that Sappho and her friends had considerable freedom to meet and engage in social and cultural activity. (It can therefore be inferred that they belonged to upper-class families that had slaves to do some or most of the "women's work.") Moreover, Archaic Greek society, at least on Lesbos, did not frown on a certain amount of female creativity and social interaction. Some of Sappho's poems were *epithalimia*, or wedding songs, which may have been performed at formal ceremonies; and some of the female relatives and professional mourners who sang laments at funerals may have composed these pieces themselves.

THE MARRIAGE INSTITUTION

Whether or not Sappho recited her poetry at weddings, it appears that she herself,

An imaginary modern depiction of Sappho reciting before a group of women who met regularly on Lesbos for social and cultural exchange.

like most Greek women, was married. Two facts of life—that the family and community could not be perpetuated without children and that the female gender bears the children—made marriage the social institution in which women played their most essential role. Most of what is known about marriage in the Archaic Age relates to the upper classes. In the early part of the age, before the emergence of centralized city-states, most marriages appear to have been arranged, with the bride and groom hailing from different communities. This habit of marrying outside the community, called exogamy, was presumably a means by which aristocrats formed political alliances with important foreign families and factions. Although the practice of exogamy continued throughout the age, after the seventh century B.C., with the ongoing rise of city-states, endogamy—marriage within the community—became increasingly common. The *polis* needed the strength of inner unity to survive and prosper. And keeping marriages within a tight circle of local families helped to ensure that unity.

An exchange of property was an important part of the marriage arrangements throughout Greek history. In Archaic times, the predominant form this property took was the *hedna,* or "bridewealth," gifts the groom gave the bride's father. Based on passages from Homer's works and other evidence, Blundell suggests the following scenario for upper-class marriages in that era:

> The process of competing for the hand of a powerful man's daughter began with an exchange of courtship gifts (or *dora*) between the suitors and the prospective father-in-law, a ritual which served to establish friendly relations between the two parties. The suitors then put in their "bids" for the young woman by making promises of bridewealth *(hedna)* which would only be accepted once the marriage had been definitely agreed. . . . The women involved in all of these marriage arrangements seem, unsurprisingly, to have had little or no say in their own futures. Clearly, among the upper classes of Archaic Greece marriage was seen as an institution that established a relationship, not so much between a woman and a man as between a father-in-law and a son-in-law.[14]

Toward the end of the Archaic Age, marriage customs, as well as many other social and legal aspects of women's lives, began undergoing significant changes, at least in Athens. By contrast, as will be seen, in some other Greek states, including Sparta, women's lives seem to have maintained more continuity during the transition to the Classic Age.

2 Women's Legal Status and Rights in the Classic Age

Although they lacked political rights and were not treated as men's equals in the Dark and Archaic Ages, women enjoyed a certain amount of freedom of movement, association, and social participation. Toward the end of Archaic times, however, the situation began to change markedly. In Athens and presumably a large number of other Greek states, increasing male anxiety about women and their roles in the community led to the introduction of laws that segregated them and closely regulated their lives. And this repressive treatment of women continued in these states throughout the Classic Age. (In Athens, it continued in large degree well beyond that period.)

It appears that these developments were linked to the consolidation of city-states and to the creation or expansion of various legal and social institutions in these states in late Archaic times. In each *polis*, male leaders became increasingly concerned about perpetuating the number and integrity of individual family groups (*oikoi*), so as to maintain a constant supply of citi-

Accompanied by their husbands, the women in this illustration enact the custom of "guest-friendship" (xenia), a relationship between residents of different political communities in which the host provided the visitor with lodging and protection.

zens, and also to ensure that the land and property of each *oikos* remained within the community (i.e., under the ownership and control of its members). This approach, they reasoned, would keep the *polis* strong and stable. Of course, men recognized that women, as the bearers of children and keepers of the home, played crucial roles in maintaining the stability of both the *oikos* and the community. On this level at least, men acknowledged women's worth and importance.

At the same time, however, community leaders in Athens and elsewhere reasoned that the most effective way to make sure that women fulfilled their roles was to oversee, regulate, and restrict them in a rigid manner. With this aim, they passed laws that strictly controlled women's social and sexual behavior and limited what they could own or inherit. The laws enacted in Athens in the early sixth century B.C. by the political and social reformer Solon, though from late Archaic times, are the best-known examples. At a time when the city's upper classes were on the brink of a civil war with the middle and lower classes, the opposing parties asked Solon, a citizen known for his wisdom and fairness, to step in and mediate. Part of his drastic reordering of the state was a new law code that included numerous restrictions on women. For example, one law placed limits on the number of women who could participate in funerals and severely regulated their behavior at such gatherings:

> The women who come to mourn at the funeral are not to leave the tomb before the men. . . . In the event that a person dies, when he is carried out,

no women should go to the house other than those polluted [rendered ritually unclean by the death]. Those polluted are the mother and wife and sisters and daughters, and in addition to these not more than five women, the daughters' children and cousins; no one else.[15]

It is important to emphasize that not all Greek *poleis* (plural for *polis*) legally restricted women to this degree in the Classic Age. In Sparta and Gortyn (in southern Crete), for instance, the laws regulating women's rights and behavior were considerably more liberal. And even if they were more liberal than most, the treatment and opportunities of women in this period varied in both kind and degree from one place to another in the Greek world.

WOMEN'S POLITICAL AND CIVIC RIGHTS AND JUSTICE

One important aspect of women's legal status in the Classic Age consisted of their political rights—or, more accurately, their lack thereof. In Athens, although women were citizens, they did not rank as *politai*, a term that means citizens but more specifically signifies "citizens with political rights." Only men were *politai*, with the rights to take part in meetings of the Assembly (the citizen body that voted leaders into office and debated and passed state legislation); hold public office; sue someone in court or sit on a jury; and serve in the military. By contrast, women were designated *astai*, meaning

This modern reconstruction shows Athens in the second century A.D., when Greece was part of the Roman Empire. As in the earlier Classic Age, women had few civil rights.

simply "members of the community." An *aste* had no direct political voice but did have the civic rights to take part in and/or benefit from the community's religious and economic institutions. Thus, for example, women played roles, often important ones, in various religious festivals.

And though women could not appear in court in direct ways—as jurors or litigants (prosecutors or defendants)—they could avail themselves of Athenian justice in indirect ways. The predominant way was for a woman's father, husband, brother, son, or other male relative to represent her interests in court. It was common, for instance, for men to prosecute or sue others in property, inheritance, adultery, and other cases directly involving women.

On occasion, a particularly desperate or assertive woman might take a more active role in fighting for justice for someone else. Such was the case of the unnamed widow[16] of a rich Athenian merchant named Diodotus, who died in battle in 409 B.C. during the bloody Peloponnesian War (fought between two blocs of city-states led by Athens and Sparta respectively). Some time after her husband's death, she studied his financial records (which incidentally indicates that she could read and compute figures), and she discovered that her father (who was also her husband's brother) had cheated her sons out of property that rightfully belonged to them. Having convinced her son-in-law to summon a meeting of all the male relatives, she boldly confronted her father. "You are their father's brother, and my father," she told him.

Even if you aren't ashamed of what men will think, you ought to fear the gods. When my husband went off to war he gave you a deposit of five talents [30,000 drachmas, a huge sum considering that the daily wage of an average worker was then about one drachma]. I am willing to swear that this is true on the lives of my sons and my younger children in any temple that you select. I am not so pathetic, and I do not think money so important that I would choose to lose my own life after swearing a false oath on my children's lives. . . . You thought it acceptable to turn your daughter's sons out of their own house in worn clothes, without shoes, with no attendant, and with no bed-clothes, and without the furniture their father left them, and without the money he had deposited with you. Meanwhile, you are bringing up the children you have had with my step-mother in great luxury. . . . You dishonor your brother's memory and think us all less important than money.[17]

We know the widow said these things because her son went on to prosecute her father in court (ca. 400 B.C.); and there, her son-in-law (who delivered the court speech because the son lacked experience in such matters) repeated her words. The son-in-law then added,

> Gentlemen of the jury, after hearing the many terrible accusations the widow had made, we were struck by what this man had done and by her speech. We saw what her sons had suffered, and we thought of their dead father, and what an unworthy guardian he had left for his estate.[18]

The outcome of the trial is unknown. But it can be fairly safely assumed that the widow's father was convicted, for in ancient Greece, as remains true in many modern societies, juries were naturally sympathetic to the plight of widows and orphans.

The case in question also partially illustrates the legal status of a woman within both her family and her community. When her husband was living, he was her *kyrios* and therefore her guardian in all legal matters. After his death, since her sons were not yet of age (legal adulthood for Athenian males began at age eighteen), her guardianship reverted to her father, who had been her *kyrios* before her marriage. In the case of a widow with young sons, once they came of age she could choose either to remain under her father's guardianship or to become the ward of one of her sons. A woman's *kyrios*, whoever he may have been, was obligated to support her financially and also to protect her, both physically and legally (in legal contracts, court cases, and so on).

LOVE AND MARRIAGE

Another legal matter to which a woman's *kyrios* routinely attended was arranging her marriage. The courting process so familiar today—namely that of a young woman meeting an eligible young man, falling in love, and deciding to get married—was largely unheard-of in ancient Athens and probably in most other Greek states. As a rule, an Athenian marriage was arranged by the girl's father or other male guardian; the leader of her clan (or *genos*, a group of families claiming descent from a common ancestor), who held more authority than a family head, might also arrange it.

Moreover, because respectable young women were rarely allowed to go out in public, and never by themselves, they did not have many chances to meet young men from other families. The few occasions when they did consisted of clan and tribal celebrations or community-wide religious festivals. But even then, contact between unmarried young men and women was surely rare, limited, and always chaperoned. So not only was marriage not a woman's decision, it was also not unusual for a young bride and groom barely to know each other before their wedding night; and social customs surrounding marriage did not encourage or even take into consideration the notion of falling in love. Some evidence suggests that romantic love between newlyweds did exist. And we cannot rule out that some husbands and wives grew to love each other over the years. But on the whole, given the impersonal, materialistic, practical nature of the system, probably a minority of couples were fortunate enough to experience genuine mutual love and respect.

As it had been in Archaic times, therefore, marriage in the Classic Age was most often a legal arrangement made by men—the prospective bride's *kyrios* and her prospective husband. The deal was made at the formal betrothal *(engue)*, usually in front of witnesses. And only after it was sealed did the arrangements for the wedding celebration *(gamos)* begin.

The lives of Athenian women were bound up with the activities and obligations of the family. This fourth-century B.C. relief shows a typical family unit consisting of father, mother, and daughter.

Following custom, shortly before the celebration the bride collected her childhood toys and the girdle that she had worn since puberty and offered them as a sacrifice to Artemis, the virgin goddess thought to protect young girls and pregnant women.

Actually, these preparations usually occurred shortly after a girl had reached puberty, for the average marriage age for Athenian girls may have been fourteen or so. By contrast, the average age for men was thirty. Modern scholars have speculated variously as to why custom dictated so great a disparity in male and female marriage ages. Some have suggested that it was a conscious and concerted male effort to maintain dominance over women, to keep young and still immature women "frozen in their development, so that they would become, as it were, perpetual children."[19] However, though this may have been the outcome that the custom produced in some cases, it is not likely that it was part of some centuries-long, nefarious male conspiracy or even the conscious intention or plan of the average man. More plausibly, as Sarah B. Pomeroy suggests,

> The necessity that the bride be a virgin, coupled with the ancient belief that young girls were lustful, made an early marriage desirable. The husband who married at thirty could well be dead at forty-five . . . leaving his wife a candidate for remarriage. . . . [Therefore] a young widow could serve as wife in a number of serial marriages. Since marriage was the preferable condition for women, and men were protective of their women, a dying husband . . . might arrange a future marriage for his wife.[20]

Once the betrothal and other preparations were complete, the formal wedding celebration took place, although it was somewhat an afterthought, for it was the betrothal that made the marriage legally binding. No complete descriptions of an ancient Greek wedding have survived. However, Sue Blundell has pieced together the following credible scenario from various literary and visual sources:

> The public part of the ceremony began with a wedding feast in the house of the bride's father. At nightfall, the partially veiled bride, the groom and the groom's best friend were carried to the couple's future home in a nuptial chariot drawn by mules, accompanied by a torchlit procession of friends and relatives singing nuptial hymns. . . . At their destination the bride was greeted by her mother-in-law, who was carrying torches, and

A Greek wedding procession is depicted on this fourth-century B.C. krater (jar used for mixing wine and water) found at Tanagra (in central Greece).

was formally conducted to the hearth, the focal point of her new home. Meanwhile, bride and groom were showered with nuts and dried fruits, emblems of fertility and prosperity, and a boy crowned with a wreath of thorns and acorns circulated among the guests distributing bread from a basket. . . . The climax of the proceedings came when the bride was led by the groom towards the bridal chamber, while a wedding hymn was sung by the guests. . . . On the following day . . . gifts were presented to the couple by the bride's father and other relatives.[21]

DOWRIES, PROPERTY, AND INHERITANCE

One of the most important aspects of the marriage union was an exchange of valuable assets at the beginning. In Archaic times (and probably long before), this had taken the form of gifts given by the groom to the bride's father (bridewealth). By the end of the Archaic Age, however, this custom had been largely replaced by one in which the property exchanged was a dowry *(proix)*—money or other valuables the bride's father provided for her financial support. The dowry was part of the complex legal customs surrounding inheritance that had evolved in Athens and various other Greek states by this time. In effect, a dowry was an indirect way for a father to leave property to his daughter without allocating her the family land, which was reserved for his sons. The money making up

the dowry was supposed to remain intact throughout her life and be used primarily for her maintenance. Her husband could use the principal—the original sum—any way he liked; but if he did, he had to pay interest on the amount he used at the high rate of 18 percent.

Also, though his son-in-law managed the dowry, the father who had given it remained a potent figure in the background, maintaining a certain amount of control over the marriage and the husband's behavior. If the couple divorced, for example, the husband had to return the entire principal of the dowry to his former wife's father or other guardian or else pay interest, once again at 18 percent, until he did so. "Thus the dowry might function as a guarantee of reasonable behavior on the part of the husband," Blundell explains.

> He himself would be deterred from pursuing a divorce for frivolous reasons, while the threat of a divorce instituted by his father-in-law, and the consequent loss of dowry, might prevent him from maltreating his wife. At the same time, the dowry would ensure a decent standard of living for a married woman. The system can therefore be linked to the increasing stress being placed . . . on the greater protection of women within marriage.[22]

The need to provide young women with dowries had many social implications. First, a father was unlikely to raise more daughters than he could afford to supply dowries for. So he might on occasion kill a female infant by leaving her outside to die of exposure. Some evidence suggests that female infants were exposed more often than male ones; however, this evidence is mostly scattered and unreliable, and at present we simply do not know how many and how often female infants were disposed of in this manner. Moreover, an unknown but perhaps sizable portion of the infants exposed were rescued by childless couples or others and thereby remained in the general population. Second, a wealthy man might supply a poorer man in his family or clan with the money needed to establish a dowry. The social obligations attending such cases, which might continue over several generations, constituted one of several ways the extended family and clan remained tight-knit. Also, a man who was heavily in debt might view marriage to a woman with a substantial dowry as a solution to his money troubles. But though this may have worked for those men who made wise investments, some who borrowed heavily on the dowry likely ended up deeper in debt than they had been before.

Dowries were only one aspect of women's involvement with property and inheritance. Although Athenian women ordinarily did not own land, they could own and dispose of certain property within their principal domain, the household, including furniture, clothes, jewelry, and slaves. (Unfortunately for them, however, their husbands could also dispose of their property, even against their wishes.) The most common way a woman acquired such property was by receiving gifts, notably her wedding gifts *(anakalupteria)*, which could be of substantial number and value, especially for members of the upper classes.

Two important questions regarding property and inheritance naturally arise. First, if a man's property customarily passed to his sons rather than to his daughters, what happened in the case

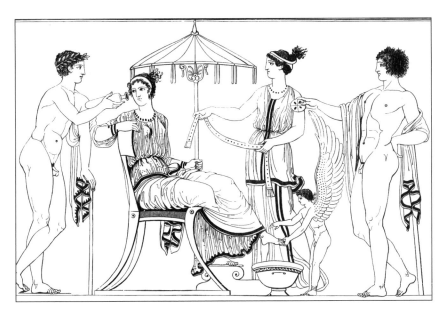

In this drawing, based on a vase painting, an Athenian bride is dressed and groomed for her wedding ceremony. As per custom, she first took a special prenuptial bath.

of a man with no sons? Second, what happened when a man had neither sons nor daughters? In both instances, the possibility of the man's *oikos* dying out and his land passing to another family would seem very real. This happened only rarely, however, for custom and law provided for such situations. First, a father with a daughter but no sons might plan ahead by adopting a son, who had to marry the daughter in order to inherit the property. When a deceased landowner left a daughter but neither natural nor adopted sons, the daughter could perpetuate the *oikos* in the role of an *epikleros* (literally meaning "with the property"). As such, she was expected to marry a male relative, one of a traditionally accepted succession of candidates (a group of relatives called the *anchisteia*). The first in line was her paternal uncle (her father's brother, who might be thirty or more years her senior), and the second was her uncle's eldest son, her cousin. (The Greeks did not view such relationships as incestuous.) Through such a marriage, the woman's father's property passed, along with her, into her male relative's custody and thereby remained within the family. In the case of a man dying with neither sons nor daughters, his property passed directly to whoever was first in line in the *anchisteia*.[23]

DIVORCE AND ADULTERY

If an Athenian marriage did not work out, divorce was an easily obtainable option with no social stigma attached. When a man initiated the procedure (a form of divorce called *apopempsis* or *ekpempsis*), he simply ordered his wife out of the house and she usually returned to the guardianship of her father, brother, or another male relative. The form of divorce initiated by the wife *(apoleipsis)* required her to get a male relative (or some other male citizen) to ask, on her behalf, for authorization from an *archon* (a high-ranking civil official). A third kind of divorce *(apheresis)* could be initiated by the wife's father, who might feel obliged to step in if her husband was abusing her or misusing her dowry. In most divorces, the husband customarily retained custody of the children; but in his view, this advantage was often balanced by the fact that he had to return the dowry, which might hurt him financially.

As is true in modern society, one common reason for divorce was adultery *(moicheia).* This was considered a serious offense because it cast doubt on the legitimacy of the children and brought shame to the whole family. A woman involved in adultery might live the rest of her life in a state of disgrace and could also lose her cherished right to take part in religious festivals. Still, her punishment was often mild compared to that of the male adulterer. This was because the woman was considered *moicheutheisa*, "corrupted" or "seduced," rather than an adulterer herself. In such situations, society viewed her as the adulterer's victim, based on the rather demeaning assumption that she was unfit to make up her own mind and was therefore easily persuaded.

By contrast, the man who had seduced her could be prosecuted by her male relatives. Moreover, an adulterer faced a high risk of death. According to an Athenian law established before Solon's time (and which he left basically intact in his reforms), a husband who actually caught another man with his wife was allowed to kill the offender on the spot; however, if someone could prove that the husband had some other motive for the killing, he could be prosecuted for murder. One of the most famous surviving Athenian law court speeches, Lysias's *For Euphiletus* (ca. 400–380 B.C.), deals with just such a situation. Euphiletus slew a man he had caught in bed with his wife, but the man's relatives accused him of plotting the whole situation leading up to the killing and prosecuted him on a charge of murder.[24]

Spartan Women

Outside of Athens and those Greek cities that shared similar social customs, the legal and social status of women in the Classic Age was somewhat more favorable. And women in a few Greek communities were allowed fairly active roles in community affairs and institutions. Stories in which the women of Argos and Tegea (both in the Peloponnesus) fought alongside their men, successfully repelling attacks by the Spartans, are likely (though not conclusively) only legends or are at least highly exaggerated.[25] But it is certainly no legend that Spartan women engaged in vigorous physical training similar to, but not as intense as, that of Spartan men and were certainly capable of fighting if the need so arose. Spartan women also enjoyed numerous rights and

privileges that many other Greek women did not.

First, it appears that women in Sparta did not simply manage the household for their husbands, as women in Athens did, but actually set the rules and largely took precedence over men in that sphere. This was because Spartan society (beginning in the Archaic Age) was built around a strict, regimented system designed to produce machinelike soldiers to man the most feared army in Greece. Spartan boys left home at age seven and up to the age of thirty or more lived in military barracks with other males. In fact, Spartan men were not allowed to reside with their wives and children until age thirty. And even then, married men were frequently absent, engaging in military training, war, hunting, and political activities; in addition, most Spartan men of all ages ate their meals with their comrades in a common mess hall. "One result of this system," says Blundell,

> was that the authority of the individual father was downgraded. . . . There can be little doubt that one effect of undermining the father's role would have been to enhance that of the mother, who by the time her husband moved into the family home would have established her preeminence there. . . . [The] radical separation of the public and private spheres . . . would have ensured that female domestic power was accepted and possibly even officially encouraged.[26]

This "female domestic power" manifested itself in a number of ways. Spartan

"WE . . . GIVE BIRTH TO MEN"

The following are just a few of the fascinating short anecdotes collected by Plutarch in his Sayings of Spartan Women *(quoted in* Plutarch on Sparta*).*

"When asked by a woman from Attica [i.e., Athens]: 'Why are you Spartan women the only ones who can rule men?', she [Gorgo] said: 'Because we are also the only ones who give birth to men.'"

"When some woman heard that her son had been saved and had escaped from the enemy, she wrote to him: 'You have been tainted by a bad reputation. Either wipe this out now or cease to exist.'"

"A Spartan who had been wounded in battle and was unable to walk made his way on all fours, ashamed of being laughed at. But his mother said: 'Son, isn't it really much better to rejoice in your courage than to feel ashamed of being laughed at by idiots?'"

"Another woman, as she was handing her son his shield and giving him some encouragement, said: 'Son, either with this or on this,' [i.e., either return victorious, carrying this shield, or lying dead on it after a fight to the death]."

An undated engraving, probably from the eighteenth century, depicts Plutarch, the famous first-century A.D. Greek biographer and moralist.

women were not largely confined in the home, as a majority of classical Athenian women were. Female Spartans were also more outspoken and assertive, often standing up, without fear, to their husbands, sons, and other men. Plutarch compiled a large collection of anecdotes about Spartan women. In one, the daughter of a Spartan king boldly interrupts his negotiations with a foreign ambassador, saying, "Father, this miserable little foreigner will ruin you completely unless you drive him out of the house pretty quickly." Another Spartan woman, Plutarch says, "After hearing that her son was a coward and unworthy of her . . . killed him when he made his appearance."[27] Such incidents would have been unthinkable in Athens and many other parts of Greece. Furthermore, Plutarch reports in his *Life of Agis*, "Spartan men were always subject to their wives and allowed them to interfere in affairs of state more than they themselves did in private ones."[28]

Spartan women could even own land. Although Spartan inheritance laws remain unclear, apparently a daughter could inherit a share of her father's land even when she had brothers, her share being half that of a male. And if she had no natural or adopted brother, she likely inherited the family property directly, without the obligation of marrying a male relative, as in the case of an Athenian *epikleros*. As a result, a good deal of land

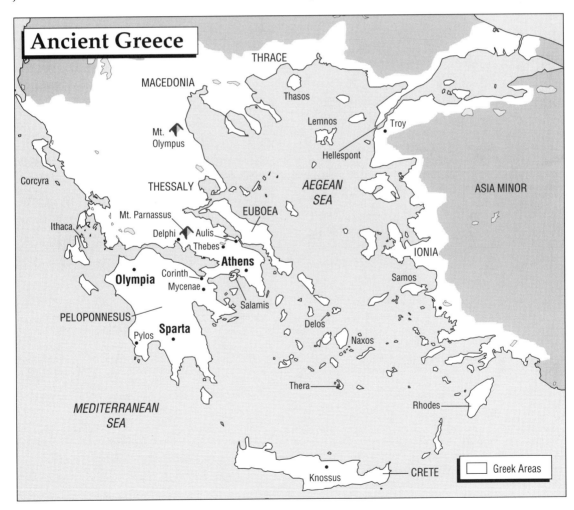

Ancient Greece

eventually fell into the hands of Spartan women. Aristotle, who complained in his *Politics* that female Spartans had entirely too much freedom, reported that in his day (the mid–fourth century B.C.) they owned fully two-fifths of the land in Sparta. And Plutarch mentions a number of wealthy Spartan women, including Archidamia, whom he calls "the richest of all the Spartans," and the mother of King Agesilaus, who "took a prominent part in public life, and with so many dependents, friends, and debtors was a figure of great influence."[29]

WOMEN IN GORTYN

Similar female property-owning privileges prevailed at Gortyn in Crete. We are fortunate to have a series of inscriptions from Gortyn that constitute the most complete surviving Greek law code. The code shows that, as in the case of women in Sparta, women in Gortyn inherited land, livestock, and/or money from their fa-

thers' estates even when they had brothers (although their shares were smaller than their brothers'). Moreover, Gortynian women retained control of their property as divorcees or widows. And in a divorce, a woman received half of the money that her property (land or livestock) had produced during the marriage, plus an extra compensatory cash payment if her husband was responsible for the divorce.

These facts about the relatively enlightened customs and laws pertaining to women in Sparta and Gortyn do not begin to tell the whole story of the status of women in these states, of course. As was true elsewhere in Greece in the Archaic and Classic Ages, Spartan and Gortynian women had no political rights and therefore had no say in government. Ultimately, they were seen as the weaker gender and were thus naturally subordinate to men. Still, comparing these customs and laws with those in Athens clearly illustrates how widely the treatment and opportunities of women varied from place to place in ancient Greece at any given time.

Chapter

3 The Home Life of Classical Greek Women

Until the advent of the modern women's movement in the nineteenth and twentieth centuries, most societies upheld the old adage that "a woman's place is in the home." Most ancient Greeks certainly saw it that way, especially the Athenians in the Classic Age, when the lives of Greek women were the most regulated and restricted. Most Greek women in this period (as well as in other periods), therefore, were wives, mothers, and housekeepers. And although men usually owned the houses and had the last word on family matters, women organized and managed the home, which was in a very real sense their principal domain. They not only supervised the children and slaves but also performed a host of essential duties, often including making all of the family's clothes, keeping the financial accounts, and paying the bills. The home was also where women birthed their children, saw to their own and their family's health care, and acquired whatever education they could.

The spheres and duties of men and women—men's outside the home and women's inside it—were already separate and clearly delineated long before the Classic Age (indeed, perhaps well before

the Bronze Age). However, it was during the Classic Age that Greek men justified this seemingly "natural" state of affairs in writing. And through those few surviving examples, we are afforded a priceless glimpse into their thinking about the opposite sex. Once more, it must be emphasized that Greek men's views of women do not necessarily reflect the views and feelings of the women themselves.

The most complete justification for the relegation of Greek women to the home appears in the *Oeconomicus* of the early fourth century B.C. Athenian soldier, philosopher, and country gentleman Xenophon (ZEN-uh-phon). Translated variously as *The Householder* or *The Management of an Estate,* the work purports to demonstrate the most efficient ways to run a country estate. It is set in the form of a dialogue, one of the chief characters being a country gentleman named Ischomachus (who is clearly a thinly disguised representation of Xenophon himself). One of the most engaging sections of the work consists of a conversation between Ischomachus and his young wife, in which the husband explains that it is nature's way for men to work outside the home and women within it:

These drawings were copied from a Greek vase. They show women engaged in various household activities, including playing music and grooming.

Since both of these domains—indoor and outdoor—require work and attention, then God, as I see it, directly made woman's nature suitable for the indoor jobs and tasks, and man's nature suitable for the outdoor ones. For he made the masculine body and mind more capable of enduring cold and heat and travel and military expeditions, which implies that he ordained the outdoor work for man; and God seems to me to have assigned the indoor work to woman, since he made the female body less capable in these respects. And knowing that he had made it the woman's natural job to feed new-born children, he appointed to her a greater facility for loving new-born infants than he did to man. And because he had assigned to the woman the work of looking after the [food] stores, God, recognizing that timidity is no disadvantage in such work, gave a larger share of fearfulness to woman than

he did to man. And knowing that it would also be necessary for the one who does the outdoor work to provide protection against potential wrongdoers, he gave him a greater share of courage. But because both sexes need to give as well as receive, he shared memory and awareness between them both, and consequently you wouldn't be able to say whether the male or the female sex has more of these. . . . So, my dear . . . we must recognize what God has assigned to each of us, and try our hardest to carry through our respective responsibilities.[30]

SEGREGATION VERSUS SECLUSION

Xenophon's explanation of why it was natural for a wife to manage the home likely reflected the view of most Greek men. Certainly in Athens, and probably in most Greek states, the majority of women

FEMALE DRESS AND GROOMING

In this excerpt from her noted volume Goddesses, Whores, Wives, and Slaves, *scholar Sarah B. Pomeroy describes the clothes, makeup, and hairdos worn by typical classical Greek women.*

"Women's clothing was, by modern standards, simple. The material used in classical times by respectable women was usually wool or linen, but prostitutes wore saffron-dyed material of gauze-like transparency. . . . A *himation,* or shawl . . . could be drawn over the head as a hood. Since the Ionic *chiton* [tunic] was confining, it tended to be the garment worn in public, and a shorter tunic was worn around the house and as a nightdress and petticoat. There was a large variety of sandals and slippers. Sandals with thongs between the toes were worn, as well as sandals with straps bound around the lower leg as far as the knee. Some women wore shoes with platform soles to increase their height. Vase paintings show women bathing themselves and tending to various parts of their toilette. . . . Cosmetics were used by housewives as well as by prostitutes. A white complexion was considered attractive, since it proved that a woman was wealthy enough not to go out in the sun. Powder of white lead was commonly used for this, and when women went outdoors they protected themselves from the sun with a parasol [small decorated umbrella]. Rouge was used on the cheeks. Although dress was simple, jewelry and hairdos could be complicated. Women wore their hair loose, surmounted by a coronet or headband, or up in a chignon [knot] or net. False curls seem to have been used sometimes. Slaves' hair, however, was usually cropped."

This bronze mirror, used for grooming by a well-to-do Greek woman, dates from the sixth or fifth century b.c.

were socially segregated from men to one degree or another much of the time. And they were also expected, as a matter of course, to perform the duties of wife and housekeeper, which meant that they spent much, if not most, of their time at home.

However, as Sue Blundell points out, "segregation is not the same thing as seclusion."[31] Even in Athens, it was apparently a respectable woman's conversing with unrelated males, either inside or outside the home, that was viewed as offensive, not the simple act of her appearing in public. (The term *respectable* is here used to differentiate married women, mothers, daughters, and other women living in traditional home environments from prostitutes, entertainers, and other women whom society viewed as disreputable.) Athenian men were extremely protective of their wives and daughters and were ever vigilant to make sure that they maintained their chastity and marital fidelity. So a husband or father saw a female relative's contact with strange men as a potentially corruptive and dangerous influence that might threaten the stability of the home and *oikos*. This is why men or slaves customarily did the shopping, for example—not because it was unseemly for women to be seen in the marketplace, but because there was the chance of their meeting and getting to know strange men there. When respectable women did leave the house, therefore, they were almost always accompanied by a slave, relative, or other chaperone.

In Athens, from which most of our evidence comes, free women had a number of possible outside destinations. They were allowed to visit friends and relatives and to attend funerals, public religious festivals (in which they played important roles), and probably the theater. On such occasions, closely watched by their husbands or chaperones, they took care to avoid conversing with unrelated men, as polite custom dictated. Women's forays outside the home were also dictated to some degree by social class and economic necessity. While women in middle- and upper-class households did not normally have outside jobs or shop or run errands, many poorer women did. "For many women of the lower classes," Blundell explains,

> complete confinement to the home would not have been feasible. Aristotle asks, "who could prevent the wives of the poor from going out when they want to?" (*Politics*). In those homes where there was no well in the courtyard, and no slave to fetch water, women would have to go to the public fountain. The female chorus in [the comic playwright] Aristophanes' *Lysistrata* speaks of the crowd that gathers round the fountain in the morning, and scenes like this are also depicted in vase paintings; there is no reason to assume that all the women represented in these are . . . slaves, aliens, or courtesans [prostitutes]. Lower-class women also went out to work, and even where they were employed indoors (for example, as midwives), they would of course have had to leave the house in order to get to their jobs.[32]

An Attic (Athenian) amphora (storage jar) from the late sixth century B.C. shows a group of women meeting at a well.

WOMEN'S QUARTERS AND DUTIES

Wherever they may have gone outside the home, for the majority of Greek women, particularly in Athens, such excursions were the exception; as a rule, they spent most of their time in their houses. Even there, their fathers and husbands were careful to keep them segregated from unrelated men. Many Greek men, especially upper-class ones, gave dinner parties and after-dinner drinking parties (*symposia*) for their male friends. Prostitutes and other female entertainers were allowed (indeed, often strongly urged) to attend, but the host's wife, daughters, and mother were barred from such gatherings. For these respectable women even to be seen by, let alone to mix with, the host's male visitors would have been a major breach of social etiquette.

At such times when strange men were around, the ladies of the house retired to the *gynaeceum* (or *gynaikonitis*), the "women's quarters." Depending on the size of the house, this consisted of one or more large utility rooms (located in the back of single-story houses and upstairs in those with two stories) in which they engaged in spinning, weaving, visiting with female guests, and other activities. The Roman writer Cornelius Nepos, who visited Athens not long after the Classic Age, found such segregation of women odd and compared it unfavorably to the customs of his own society:

> Many actions are seemly according to our [the Roman] code which the Greeks look upon as shameful. For instance, what Roman would blush to take his wife to a dinner-party? What matron does not frequent the front rooms of her dwelling and show herself in public? But it is very different in [Athens]; for there a woman is not admitted to a dinner-party, unless relatives only are present, and she keeps to the more retired part of the house called "the women's apartment," to which no man has access who is not near of kin.[33]

Yet although they kept to their quarters while the master was entertaining guests, the women almost certainly had the run of the house the rest of the time. A wife had important duties, after all, that she could not have performed if she were locked away all day in the *gynaeceum.* In fact, it was the large number of these duties, much more than any forced confinement by men, that kept most women so often at home. In another passage from *Lysistrata,* Aristophanes has a female character say, "It's hard for women, you know, to get away [from the house]. There's so much to do. Husbands to be patted and put in good tempers, servants to be [kept track of], children washed or soothed . . . or fed."[34] In addition to overseeing the children and servants, paying the bills, and spinning and weaving, housewives and mothers typically had to help prepare the meals and in general keep the home clean and well organized. The common wisdom, at least as portrayed and perpetuated by men, was that performing these duties faithfully and well was the key not only to a well-ordered household but also to a woman's ultimate worth and happiness. In his *Oeconomicus,* Xenophon has Ischomachus tell his wife,

> You will have to stay indoors and send out the servants who have outside jobs, and oversee those with indoor jobs. You must receive the produce that is brought in from outside and distribute as much of it as needs dispensing; but . . . you must look ahead and make sure that the outgoings [moneys to pay the bills] assigned for the year are not dispensed in a month. When wool is brought in to you, you must try to make certain that those who need clothes get them. And you must try to ensure that the grain is made into edible provisions. One of your responsibilities, however . . . will probably seem rather unpleasant. When any servant is ill, you must make sure that he is thoroughly looked after. . . . Some of your specific responsibilities will be gratifying, such as getting a servant who is ignorant of spinning, teaching it to her, and doubling her value to you . . . or having the right to reward those in your household who are disciplined and helpful, and to punish anyone who turns out to be bad. And the most gratifying thing of all will be if you turn out to be better than me, and make me your servant. . . . As you grow older, you will have

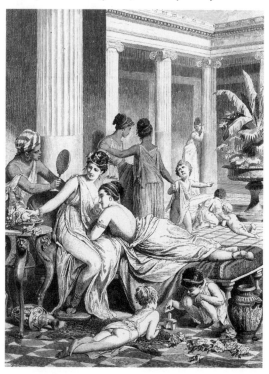

This modern depiction of the women's quarters of an Athenian wife considerably exaggerates the size, splendor, and frivolous use of such facilities.

These perfume containers, made of terracotta (fired clay) and richly orna-
mented, originally belonged to a well-to-do fourth-century B.C. Greek woman.

more standing in the household, in proportion to the increase in your value to me as a partner and to our children as a protector of the home. For it is virtue rather than the physical beauty of youth that increases true goodness in human life.[35]

EDUCATING YOUNG WOMEN AT HOME

The fact that women often kept track of the household finances and paid the bills indicates that some women were at least partially educated. Those fathers and husbands who considered the household finances a regular duty of the lady of the house may have taught their daughters and wives this skill themselves. But probably more often it was one of several skills, including spinning, weaving, and so on, passed down from mother to daughter. Vase paintings and other evidence show that some Athenian women could also read and write. And this learning must also have come from the mother (or possibly in rare cases from the father) in the home, for in Athens girls did not receive formal educations in schools, as boys did. Athenian girls were also deprived of athletic training, a regular feature of boys' schooling.

As to why Athenian women did not receive formal schooling, first and foremost society did not perceive any compelling need for it. On the one hand, the primary means of communication in ancient Greece was the spoken word, which meant that illiteracy was generally not a significant handicap; and indeed, throughout Greece a large portion of men as well as women,

A Woman Eager to Learn

At least a few classical Greek women went to great pains to educate themselves, as indicated in this tract by an unknown writer (quoted in Lefkowitz's and Fant's sourcebook). The woman the author describes was the mother of Philip II, king of the northern Greek kingdom of Macedonia.

"We ought therefore to try every appropriate means of disciplining our children, following the example of Eurydice. She was an Illyrian and a complete barbarian, but late in life she became involved in education because of her children's studies. The epigram she set up to the Muses [goddesses who inspired creativity and intellectual activity] provides adequate documentation of her love for her children: 'Eurydice . . . set up this tablet when she had satisfied her desire to become learned; for she worked hard to learn letters, the repository of speech, because she was a mother of growing sons.'"

This original Greek statue shows a young woman reading a book. Historical evidence indicates that some women were taught to read and write, probably most often by their mothers.

especially in the poorer classes, were likely illiterate. On the other hand, tradition had long assigned women mainly household duties, which required no literacy or athletic skills, whereas it was expected that some men would enter politics, intellectual pursuits, and athletic competitions, which did require such skills.

Whatever the reasons may have been that women, on the whole, were less educated than men, that fact almost surely reinforced the traditional perception that women were intellectually inferior to men. Also, despite whether they accepted this notion, some men evidently saw educated women as potentially dangerous. In Athens, the male-dominated order rested in large degree on the segregation of male and female spheres, and an educated woman might be seen as crossing over into the male sphere and thereby threatening that order. In the fourth century B.C. (the second half of the Classic Age), Athenian schoolboys were regularly taught the maxim "A man who teaches a woman to write should recognize that he is providing poison to an asp [a deadly snake]."[36] Apparently some men even consciously tried to keep their women ignorant. As Xenophon's Ischomachus remarks of his wife, "She wasn't yet fifteen years old when she came to me, and in her life up till then considerable care had been taken that she should see and hear and discover as little as possible."[37]

In Sparta, by contrast, young women received both athletic and intellectual training. According to Xenophon, who lived among the Spartans for many years,[38] physical fitness was seen to be as important for girls as for boys; Spartan girls, he tells us, ran footraces and competed in trials of strength. Plutarch adds that these young women also wrestled and threw the discus and javelin. "Thereby," he says, "their children in embryo would make a strong start in strong bodies and would develop better,

This painting on an Attic (Athenian) cup shows a woman playing a flute for a man. It is unclear whether the artist meant to depict an Athenian or a Spartan woman.

while the women themselves would also bear their pregnancies with vigor and would meet the challenge of childbirth in a successful, relaxed way."[39]

In addition, Plato mentions that Spartan girls were trained in music and other arts and that both Spartan and Gortynian girls prided themselves on their intellectual development as much as their men did. He does not elaborate, so we do not know the nature and extent of this development. But it must have included reading and writing, which comprise the fundamental basis for any intellectual endeavor. Corroborating this is the evidence that in the Classic Age Sparta and some other cities in the Peloponnesus produced female poets, who, though most of their works have not survived, gained considerable reputations in their own time. Aristophanes mentions a Spartan poet named Cleitagora; another female poet, Telesilla, hailed from Argos (in the northeastern Peloponnesus); and still another, Praxilla, lived in Sicyon (in the northern Peloponnesus). Three other female poets of the Classic Age are known: Myrtis and Corinna, both from Boeotia (the region lying directly north of Athens), and Erinna, from Telos (an island off the coast of Asia Minor). Because all of these accomplished women were non-Athenians, and also because we know of no classical female Athenian poet, it strongly suggests that Athens's complete exclusion of women from formal education was unusually restrictive for a Greek state.

Puberty and Pregnancy

Another activity that women engaged in at home was, by its very nature, exclusively female—namely, childbirth. The entire reproductive process, from the onset of female puberty to the actual delivery of a child, was determined in large degree by the common medical wisdom of the day. Unfortunately, that so-called wisdom was riddled with what are now known to be either old wives' tales or mistaken theories proposed by Greek doctors. Many of these theories were recorded in the writings of the medical school founded by Hippocrates (now called "the Father of Medicine"), which flourished on the Greek island of Cos (near the coast of Asia Minor) in the fifth and fourth centuries B.C.

The treatise titled *On Virgins*, for example, states that when a girl reaches puberty and starts having her period, she is in danger of having hallucinations and acting irrationally. This is because she has not yet had sexual intercourse; and the mouth of her womb is therefore "unopened," forcing most of the blood to move back up to her heart and lungs, making her feverish and prone to rash judgments. The proper treatment, according to Hippocratic theory, is for the girl to have intercourse and undergo her first pregnancy, which will "open up" her body to "normal" functioning and development. These ideas obviously reinforced the already common practice of forcing young girls into marriage very soon after they reached puberty.

Once a young woman became pregnant, she was subject to other common folk beliefs. One was that her condition made her much more vulnerable to "pollution," that is, religious taint or impurity. Therefore, she should try to avoid contact with the dead, criminals, childbirth, or other persons and situations thought to be impure, lest they infect her. (People who took part in funerals or childbirth washed themselves afterward in cleansing rituals; also, pregnant women were not seen as a *source* of pollution, so could still visit religious sanctuaries.)

Childbirth and Child Loss

A woman usually gave birth in her home, likely in the women's quarters, if the house had such an area, or in her bedroom. As a rule, the baby was delivered

A Greek Doctor Attempts to Explain Miscarriages

This excerpt from one of the Hippocratic medical writings, Diseases of Women *(quoted in Lefkowitz's and Fant's sourcebook) discusses some of the perceived reasons for pregnant women miscarrying.*

"Some women conceive a child easily, but are not able to carry it full term; the children are lost through miscarriage in the third or fourth month—even though the woman has suffered no physical injury nor eaten the wrong kind of food. In such women the cause of the circumstances mentioned is especially when the womb releases matter which would make the embryo grow. The woman's bowels become upset; weakness, high fever, and lack of appetite affect them during the time in which they are aborting their children. The following is also a cause, namely if the womb is smooth—either naturally or due to the presence of lacerations in the womb. Now if the womb is smooth, sometimes the membranes which envelop the child are detached from the womb when the child begins to move. . . . If the menses [menstrual discharges] flow in these women, they come copiously [abundantly]. Occasionally some of these women carry their embryos to full term, and when such women are cared for, they have hope of a normal birth."

by a midwife *(maia)*, aided by female relatives and friends. Blundell here summarizes the main points of what little is known about the childbirth procedure:

It seems that women usually gave birth in a seated position, either on a birthing stool, or, in an emergency, on the lap of one of the helpers. It was probably unusual for a woman to be delivered lying down, but it was certainly not unknown. A number of Hippocratic sources refer to the use of drugs to speed up delivery . . . and sometimes labor would have

to be induced; one Hippocratic author describes a rather violent method whereby four female assistants seize the woman by the legs and arms and give her at least ten firm shakes, then place her on a bed with her legs in the air and subject her to more shaking by the shoulders. . . . At the moment of birth the mother's helpers uttered a ritual cry of joy. . . . Once the afterbirth [placenta] had been expelled, mother and child were given a ritual bath to cleanse them of the defilement [ritual pollution] of the birth process.[40]

Soon after the child was delivered in this manner, the parents announced the birth to the community by pinning an olive stem to the door if it was a boy or a piece of wool if it was a girl. And sometime

A statue of Artemis, goddess of the moon, animals, and the hunt, who also aided pregnant women.

shortly afterward, the new mother visited a shrine dedicated either to Artemis (who was thought to aid women in childbirth) or Ilithyia, the goddess of childbirth. There, the woman thanked the deity by offering her a finely made piece of clothing.

Similar ritual offerings were also made by family members in memory of those women who died in childbirth. The percentage of Greek women who fell into this unfortunate category is unknown, but most modern scholars think that 10 to 20 percent is probable, due mainly to the high proportion of teenage mothers (who even today run a higher risk of complications in pregnancy and birth) and widespread ignorance about proper hygiene. That this maternal mortality rate is frighteningly high becomes plain when compared to that in the United States today, where only one woman in ten thousand (.01 percent) dies in childbirth.

As for infant mortality, scholar Mark Golden (noted for his studies of ancient Greek children) estimates that as many as 25 to 35 percent of children died in their first year of life (as compared to less than 1 percent in the United States today).[41] This suggests that a large majority of Greek women must have experienced the loss of at least one child. From such grim statistics, some modern scholars have hypothesized that many Greek women must have conditioned themselves not to feel such losses too strongly; therefore, perhaps maternal love (and maybe paternal love, too) was not as strong as it is in developed modern societies. However, numerous references to the anguish felt by

Modern sculptor Hiram Powers created this statue of a female Greek slave. The subject's nudity is artistic license; slaves in Greece were as fully clothed as free people.

mothers on losing a child can be found in the surviving Athenian sources. These have led Golden to conclude that "the weight of the evidence seems overwhelmingly to favor the proposition that the Athenians loved their children and grieved for them deeply when they died."[42]

SLAVES

So far, attention has been focused on free wives and mothers, the "ladies of the house," so to speak, in Greek society; however, other sorts of women, both free and unfree, lived in many Greek homes. The unfree variety were, of course, house slaves. The number of slaves per household in the Classic Age is much disputed by scholars, but it was probably one or two in homes of average means and perhaps as many as ten or more in well-to-do homes. Of these slaves, at least half, and likely a higher proportion than that, were women. They helped with the cooking and cleaning and performed whatever tasks their owners considered the most menial.

Surviving sources indicate that most house slaves were generally well treated and were sometimes even loved like members of the family. And a few were eventually granted their freedom. However, it is unknown what proportion of those freed were women.

4 The Community Roles and Activities of Classical Greek Women

Although for a variety of reasons the majority of classical Greek women, especially Athenian ones, spent most of their time in the home, they were still active members of their communities. And as such, they fulfilled certain traditional social roles and functions and took part in a range of activities outside the home. This range was significantly more limited than that open to men, of course. Moreover, female forays outside the home were viewed as socially acceptable only at certain times and under certain conditions. The male-controlled community, particularly in more conservative states like Athens, segregated and regulated women just as much outside the home as within it. Yet Greek women's participation in and contributions to community and public life were by no means trivial. Women worked in a fairly wide variety of outside occupations, some (like midwives and prostitutes) then considered fundamental to everyday life, and they played key roles in public religious worship, one of the two main areas (along with childbirth) in which they could supercede men.

The worshipers congregating outside the temple in this modern reconstruction include several women. Though they spent much of their time at home, women took part in some community activities, including religious festivals.

COMMON FEMALE OCCUPATIONS

In Athens, most of the women who worked outside the home were either poor citizen women (*astai*) or noncitizens, both free and slave. The noncitizens included female *metics* (or *metoikoi*, foreigners—either Greeks from other *poleis* or non-Greeks—residing in Athens), slaves, and freedwomen (former slaves who had gained their freedom and thereby attained the same legal status as *metics*). There was no particular stigma attached to these women working, for it was widely understood that they had no other choice in order to survive, and socially speaking, it was expected of them. By contrast, for middle-and upper-class citizen women to work outside the home was viewed as socially unacceptable.

Through remarks made in various written sources, modern historians know of some of the occupations of Athenian women (and presumably most of those of the other Greek women who worked). A court speech written by the fourth-century B.C. orator Demosthenes, for instance, reveals that citizen women worked as grape pickers. And in *Lysistrata*, Aristophanes mentions women, presumably citizens, working as barmaids and selling bread, garlic, and other groceries in the marketplace. Apparently it was acceptable for women to sell these and other items in public as long as the value of the items was small. (Athenian law stated that women and minors could not engage in transactions or contracts valued at more than a *medimnus*, roughly the amount of barley that would sustain an average family for six days.) Citizen women also took jobs as midwives, nursemaids (wet nurses for babies), laundresses, woolworkers, and as other textile workers.

Female *metics* and freedwomen likely held some or all of these same jobs, working right alongside poor citizen women; evidence suggests that the financial status and lifestyles of women in all of these groups were similar and that they mingled professionally (and perhaps socially) to one degree or another. Whether citizen women received more pay than noncitizens for the same jobs is unclear. A crucial source revealing some of the major occupations of Athenian freedwomen consists of inscriptions that some of these women made at the time of their manumission (release from slavery). In giving thanks to Athena (not only Athens's patron goddess but also goddess of urban arts and crafts), they stated their names and professions, for example: "Onesime, sesame seed–seller . . . Lampris, wet nurse . . . Lyde, woolworker . . . Thraitta, grocer . . . Malthace, woolworker (with her three children)."[43] Among the other occupations so listed are perfume vendor, cloak seller, salt vendor, shoe seller, honey seller, horse tender, and flute player.

Epitaphs on gravestones also reveal some female professions, midwife being a common one. Decidedly more uncommon is the case of a fourth-century B.C. Athenian woman, whose epitaph reads: "Phanostrate, a midwife and physician, lies here. She caused pain to none, and all lamented her death."[44] There is no way of knowing what classes or genders of

*A modern artist's conception of part of the marketplace (*agora*) at Athens. Poorer women were allowed to sell various inexpensive goods in the* agora.

people she treated or how the community accepted her, but it is certain that she was exceptional, for female doctors were rare, especially in conservative Athens, the role of physician being traditionally a male one. Also perhaps exceptional was the woman depicted in a fifth-century B.C. Athenian vase painting. In a scene showing a potter's workshop, she sits, not far from some male workers, painting a large pot.[45] Most likely she is the wife or daughter (or maybe a slave) of a *metic* since most of the artisans in Athens were *metics*. Although such noncitizen female artisans may in fact have been unusual, there is the chance that they were not all that uncommon and that they were simply not very often depicted in art or mentioned in inscriptions.

PROSTITUTION—A SOCIAL DOUBLE STANDARD

In Athens, for poor, noncitizen, or slave women to work as midwives, laundresses, food sellers, and so on was definitely not as socially desirable or respectable a situation as being a wife and mother in a "good" home. Yet at least these working women labored in what society viewed as morally acceptable occupations. On the other hand, some women worked in professions that were widely seen as disreputable—as prostitutes, both high class (courtesans) and common, and as entertainers. These lines of work were not illegal. In fact, they were ever-present and thriving realities of life in all Greek cities.

This reflects a clear double standard of male-dominated Greek society—namely, that society looked down on prostitutes and entertainers; yet men unashamedly availed themselves of their services on a regular basis. Indeed, in the eyes of some men, they were as indispensable as their wives in maintaining a pleasant, well-ordered life. In his court speech *Against Neaera*, Demosthenes captured this chauvinistic social reality in a phrase often quoted by modern scholars: "Courtesans we keep for pleasure, concubines for daily attendance upon our person, but wives for the procreation of legitimate children and to be our faithful housekeepers."[46] Moreover, it was not simply a matter of polite society winking at behavior it viewed as immoral; in Athens (and probably most other Greek cities), state officials actually set the maximum prices that prostitutes could charge and taxed their income.

As they do today, prostitutes in ancient Greece ranged from inexpensive "low-class" types who worked in brothels to high-priced, often highly educated "companions" who came to men's homes. The common prostitutes (*pornai*) were most often found in "red-light" districts, areas in which they and other social outcasts congregated; in Athens, these were the Ceramicus (where most of the potters' shops were located) and sections of the city's port, Piraeus. Two kinds of *pornai*

could be found in these areas—those who lived and worked in brothels and the perhaps slightly higher-class streetwalkers. Those in the brothels were probably most often slaves owned by the men who ran these establishments; meanwhile, the streetwalkers were either freedwomen, *metics*, or, on occasion, citizen women who had been forced into the profession by extreme poverty or other sad circumstances. Few substantial descriptions of common Greek prostitutes have survived. But one, from a fragment of a work by the fourth-century B.C. comic playwright Xenarchus, confirms that they were very much like their modern counterparts:

> There are young ladies here at the brothels who are most amenable, ladies you are not banned from looking at as they sun-bathe with bare breasts, stripped for action in semi-circular ranks; and from among these ladies you can select whichever one you like: thin, fat, round, tall, short, young, old, middle-aged or past it. . . . With these girls you're the one that gets grabbed. They positively pull you inside, calling the old men "Little Daddies" and the younger ones "Little Brothers." And any one of them is available, without risk, without expense, in the daytime, in the evening, any way you want it.[47]

As for the streetwalkers, many may have been occasionally or permanently homeless, as suggested by some of their common nicknames, preserved in brief references in comedies and other ancient sources: Peripolas ("Wanderer"), Gephuris ("Bridge-Woman"), Spodesilaura ("Alley-Walker"), and Dromas ("Runner").[48]

PROFESSIONAL COMPANIONS AND ENTERTAINERS

By contrast, the far higher-class courtesans (*hetairai*, translated literally as "companions"), at what Sue Blundell calls "the top end of the sexual market,"[49] had no trouble finding comfortable lodgings. In Athens they were most often foreigners (and therefore noncitizens) who earned high wages entertaining men either in rented houses or rooms (paid for by either the men or the courtesans themselves) or in the men's homes. As Eva Cantarella explains, one important reason that a *hetaira* commanded higher status and fees than ordinary prostitutes was that she provided men with more than just sex:

> More educated than a woman destined for marriage, and intended "professionally" to accompany men where wives and concubines could not go, the *hetaira* was a sort of remedy provided by a society of men which, having segregated its women, still considered that the company of some of them could enliven their social activities, meetings among friends, and discussions which their wives, even if they had been allowed to take part, would not have been able to sustain. Enter the *hetaira*, who was paid for a relationship (including sex) which was neither exclusive

nor merely occasional, as indicated by her name, which means "companion." This relationship was meant to be somehow gratifying to the man, even on the intellectual level, and was thus completely different from men's relationships with either wives or prostitutes.[50]

Indeed, in a society that frowned on female independence and excluded women from formal education, courtesans were the most economically independent women around and were far better educated than the average man. "Courtesans were among the most educated people of the day," says University of Louisville scholar Robert B. Kebric, "for their clients were the elite of society. . . . Philosophy, history, politics, science, art, and literature were all necessary tools if a courtesan expected to be successful."[51]

One very intelligent, educated, and successful courtesan became the most famous woman in fifth-century B.C. Athens. Aspasia, who hailed from Miletus (on the western coast of Asia Minor), became the mistress of Pericles, the leading Athenian statesmen of the age. After he divorced his wife (in the 440s B.C.), Aspasia moved in with him, and they remained together as unofficial husband and wife until his death in 429. Evidently it was a relationship of genuine love and respect, much as in the modern ideal, which made it extremely unusual for its time and place. They also had a child together.[52] And Aspasia may actually have influenced some of his political decisions. In his *Life of Pericles*, Plutarch refers to:

ASPASIA THE INTELLECTUAL

Though most ancient Greek men did not believe or else did not like to admit that a woman could be the intellectual equal of a man, brief passages in various Greek and Roman works attest that Aspasia was well known for her intellectual endeavors. From his informative book Greek People, *University of Louisville scholar Robert B. Kebric here explores this side of her character.*

"Her relationship with Pericles would have placed Aspasia in contact, if she were not already, with some of the greatest freethinkers and intellectuals of the day in Athens. Pericles . . . liked to associate with such types. . . . Aspasia's apparent receptiveness to new ideas and intellectual inquiry was something the two had in common. . . . Since Aspasia is credited with having rather formidable rhetorical skills [rhetoric was the art of persuasive speech], she would have acquired some of her training from one or more of the sophists ('wise men') present in Athens at the time. . . . They were mostly itinerant teachers, who traveled from city to city teaching, for a fee, a variety of subjects—but mostly oratory and those skills that enhanced one's chances for material success. . . . We definitely know that Aspasia had a long and lasting friendship with Socrates, who must have been about her age. The diminutive [small] man with the homely face is generally regarded as the father of Western philosophy. He was apparently fascinated with the intellectual capabilities of Aspasia. . . . There was certainly some common intellectual ground between the two—even detractors called her a 'Socratic' and Plato [Socrates' pupil] playfully portrayed her as the philosopher's instructor—and we must suppose that Aspasia had some role in helping Socrates refine his own ideas—including those about women."

A bust of Pericles, the greatest Athenian statesman of the fifth century B.C., with whom Aspasia lived until his death in 429.

the extraordinary art or power this woman exercised, which enabled her to captivate the leading statesmen of the day. . . . [Pericles] was attracted to Aspasia mainly because of her rare political wisdom . . . [and his] attachment to [her] seems to have been a . . . passionate affair. [After his divorce] when they [he and his wife] found each other incompatible, Pericles legally handed her over to another man with her own consent and himself lived with Aspasia, whom he loved dearly. . . . Every day, when he went out to the marketplace and returned, he greeted her with a kiss.[53]

The social situation Aspasia managed to acquire was exceptional, of course. More commonly, *hetairai* spent only brief periods in respectable homes, as outside entertainers brought in to enliven all-male dinner parties and *symposia*. Those hosts who could afford it sometimes also hired other kinds of female entertainers—dancers, musicians, and the like. Xenophon describes two of them in his work appropriately titled *The Symposium*:

> When the table had been removed . . . a Syracusan came in to provide entertainment. He had with him a girl who was an expert pipe-player, another who was an acrobatic dancer, and a very attractive boy who both played the lyre [harp] and danced extremely well. The man made a living by exhibiting these [performers] . . . as a novelty. . . . [When the acrobatic dancer was ready to perform,] the other girl began to play for her on the pipes, and

A carved stone relief found in Greece depicts a dancer. Dancers and other entertainers routinely performed at upper-class dinner and drinking parties.

a man standing by the dancer handed her hoops until she had twelve. She took them and threw them spinning up into the air as she danced, judging how high to throw them so as to catch them in time with the music. . . . Next a circular frame was brought in, closely set around with upright sword-blades, and the dancer turned somersaults into this and out again over the blades, so that the spectators were afraid that she would hurt herself; but she went through her performance confidently and safely.[54]

Such performers were likely either slaves owned by (or former slaves who, after gaining their freedom, continued to work for) men, like Xenophon's Syracusan, who traveled from city to city with troupes of entertainers for hire.

WOMEN IN RELIGIOUS RITUAL

Far more socially acceptable than their working, Greek women's participation in religious rites and observances constituted their most important activity outside the home. "The politically oppressed," scholars Mary R. Lefkowitz and Maureen B. Fant point out,

> often turn to ecstasy [here meaning religious rapture] as a temporary means of possessing the power they otherwise lack. [In ancient Greece] orgiastic ritual, secret cults, trances, and magic provided such outlets, especially for women, who could not justify meeting together for any other purpose.[55]

The most visible female religious role was that of priestess *(hiereia)*. As a rule, men officiated as priests in the sanctuaries (religious sites, each consisting of a temple and its sacred grounds) of male gods, and women were the chief religious figures in those of female deities. (All sanctuaries also had a number of subordinate individuals, both male and female, who assisted in various rituals or saw to the site's upkeep; they also often bore the title of priest or priestess.) In Athens, for instance, where priestess was the only public office a woman could hold, the head of the cult (religious congregation) of the city's patron goddess, Athena, was a high priestess. She held her position, which passed through the female line of an aristocratic clan, the Eteoboutadai, for life.[56] There were, in addition, many other Athenian cults and religious festivals that featured priestesses or female worshipers with prominent roles or functions.

Some of these roles and functions are illustrated in women's participation in

A priestess burning incense is depicted in this portion of a Greek wall painting. In Athens, the position of priestess was the only public office a woman could hold.

THE RELIGIOUS DUTIES OF YOUNG GIRLS

In his famous play Lysistrata, *the comic playwright Aristophanes included a short speech by the female chorus (quoted here from Moses Hadas's translation) that reveals some of the common religious duties of the city's aristocratic young girls.*

"All you fellow-citizens, hark to me while I tell what will aid Athens well. Just as is right, for I have been a sharer in all the lavish splendor of the proud city. I bore the holy vessels at seven [as *arrephoroi*, in service to Athena on the Acropolis, they took part in a ceremony in which they carried certain sacred objects on their heads], then I pounded barley at the age of ten [to make a special cake for a goddess, possibly Demeter], and clad in yellow robes soon after this I was Little Bear [*arktos*, a young girl in service for a year] to Brauronian Artemis [i.e., at Artemis's sanctuary at Brauron, southeast of Athens]; then wearing a necklace of figs, grown tall and pretty, I was a basket-bearer [as *kanephoroi*, they marched in processions carrying baskets containing sacred objects]."

A priestess at Delphi (in central Greece) receives offerings for the god Apollo, whose shrine there contained the ancient world's most famous oracle.

Athens's most important religious festival—the Panathenaea, translated roughly as "Rites of All Athenians." Dedicated to Athena and made up of religious ceremonies, feasts, and musical and athletic contests, it was held annually in midsummer but was celebrated with special pomp every fourth year. Most scholars believe it began with a huge and stately procession that wound its way through the city to the summit of the Acropolis. The marchers represented all social classes and groups, including *metics*, freedmen and slaves, soldiers, women, and children (both boys and girls). "Of particular note" among these children, Sarah B. Pomeroy observes,

> are the young girls, called *kanephoroi*, who carried sacred baskets in the procession. [They] were virgins selected from noble families. Their virginity was a potent factor in securing the propitious [beneficial] use of the sacred offerings and sacrificial instruments carried in their baskets. To prevent the candidate from participating in this event was to cast aspersions on her reputation.[57]

Women also tended to the Panathenaea's principal single element—the *peplos*, Athena's sacred robe. Months before, the goddess's high priestess had begun the creation of a new robe by setting up the loom. She was assisted by four girls between the ages of seven and eleven, the *arrephoroi*, who lived on the Acropolis for a year while in special service to the goddess. Two or more other maidens, the *ergastinai*, then proceeded to weave the robe. This garment was eventually draped around a wooden statue of Athena that rested in the Erechtheum temple, replacing the one made for the prior festival. (Following the Panathenaea, a group of women from the Athenian clan Praxiergidai took charge of

A section of the Parthenon's Ionic frieze, designed by Phidias, the greatest sculptor of ancient times, shows horsemen taking part in the Panathenaea.

the robe and later, in a ceremony called the Plynteria, which took place in April, they washed and dressed the statue.)

In another important Athenian festival (which was also celebrated in other parts of Greece)—the Thesmophoria, which was held in October in honor of Demeter, an agricultural goddess—women were the only worshipers allowed to take part. The festival was further limited to citizen women, who met for three days on the Pnyx Hill (also the site of the Assembly's meetings). They slept in makeshift huts and held various rituals, including reenactments of events from the goddess's principal myth and sacrifices and feasts, all intended to ensure a plentiful harvest of cereal crops.

The Famous Oracle

The most famous of all the Greek women involved in religious rituals were not Athenians but rather inhabitants of Phokis, a region (and city-state) in central Greece just north of the Gulf of Corinth. This was the location of the sanctuary of Apollo, the god of light, healing, and the arts, and its renowned oracle. The oracle was a priestess who was thought to be a medium between the gods and humans and was therefore able to relay divine answers from Apollo to the questions asked by the many religious pilgrims who visited his temple. (The sacred site and the messages the priestess delivered were also referred to as oracles.)

The Delphic oracle was one of two notable exceptions to the rule about male priests officiating at sanctuaries of male gods (the other being the female oracle of Zeus at Dodona in northwestern Greece). A priestess at Delphi bore the title of Pythia, after *Pythios* in Apollo Pythios, one of the most common names for the god. The noted Greek archaeologist Manolis Andronicos here summarizes what is known about the priestess's personal attributes and her delivery of prophecy:

> The Pythia was a woman over 50 years old [in the Classic Age; some ancient sources say that in earlier times she had been a young virgin]. She was not necessarily a virgin, but from the moment she undertook this highest of duties—serving the god— she was under the obligation to abandon her husband and children, to move into a house destined for her alone, within the sacred precinct [sanctuary], to be chaste and irreproachable, and to observe certain religious rules. In spite of her age, she wore the garments of a young girl, as a mark of the virginal purity of her life. We do not know how the Pythia was selected; but it is quite certain that she did not have to belong to a noble family . . . nor did she have to go through special training and education. She was a simple, ordinary peasant-woman, without any distinguishing mark until the moment Apollo allowed his inspiration to descend upon her. In the beginning there was only one Pythia; but when the requirements of the oracle grew more numerous, two more Pythias

ORACLES AND THE FATES OF NATIONS

The messages given by the oracle at Delphi were often trivial, affecting only the life and fortunes of a pilgrim who visited the shrine and asked a question. Sometimes, however, a message affected or foretold the fate of an entire city-state, kingdom, or people. One of the most famous examples occurred in 546 B.C. as the Persians were about to invade Lydia, a kingdom encompassing most of western Asia Minor. The Lydian king, Croesus, sent a messenger to Delphi to consult Apollo's oracle about whether he was wise to fight the Persians. The oracle stated that if he crossed the Halys River and attacked the invaders, he would destroy a great empire. Filled with confidence, he attacked, but to his surprise he was defeated. He had forgotten the riddle-like nature of oracular advice and failed to consider that the "great empire" that would be destroyed might be his own.

The Delphic oracle gave another fateful piece of advice in 630 B.C. to the residents of the Aegean island of Thera, which was in the throes of a devastating famine. The oracle instructed the Therans to abandon their home and establish a colony on the northern coast of Africa. Some of the people followed this advice, and the new colony became very prosperous.

were added. . . . It was upon [Apollo's throne, the "sacred tripod"] that the Pythia sat in order to become the god's instrument. It was enough for her to take Apollo's place, to shed her ordinary identity, fall into a trance, and deliver the divine messages in a series of mysterious, inarticulate cries. . . . [When a pilgrim entered to ask a question, she] was already seated on the tripod in the *adyton,* or inner shrine. The *prophetai* [priests who aided her; singular is *prophetes*] stood nearby and the pilgrim . . . sat in a corner at some distance from her, having already posed his question to one of the *prophetai,* either in writing or orally. The Pythia, hidden by some kind of partition, was not visible to anyone. The *prophetes* put the question to her and she would give the god's response, deep in her trance. This was apparently unintelligible to others, but the *prophetes* was able to comprehend it and write it down. . . . It was this written reply that was handed over to the pilgrim.[58]

The answers given by the Delphic oracle were invariably ambiguous, obscure, and/or open to various interpretations. When her message pertained to the possible fate of a city or kingdom, therefore, both religious and civil authorities argued heatedly over its meaning and if and how they should react to it.

WOMEN'S ATHLETICS

Religious ceremonies also afforded a few Greek women the opportunity to take

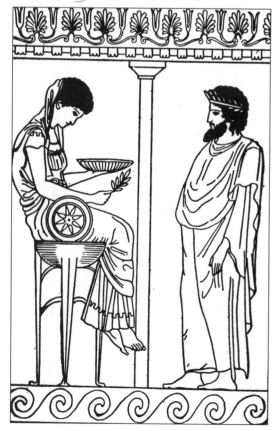

A drawing copied from a vase painting shows a religious pilgrim consulting the Delphic oracle.

part in a public activity generally dominated by men—namely, athletic competition. (All athletic games were connected to sacred festivals honoring a god or gods.) In conservative Athens, women were not allowed to compete in the games held at the Panathenaea and other festivals. But not surprisingly, the situation was quite different in Sparta, where, as Xenophon, Plutarch, Pausanias, and other ancient writers record, they took part in numerous athletic events. For example, Spartan women competed in a race for two-horse chariots held at the local festival honoring Apollo and Hyacinthus (Apollo's friend, who died tragically). And an inscription reveals that women were actually in charge of these games: "officers and overseers for life of the most sacred games of the Hyacinthia."[59] Spartan women may also have competed at times alongside Spartan men in some games; and both genders may have done so in the nude, although these points remain uncertain.

By contrast, in larger, more international athletic games, such as those held at Olympia, Delphi, and a few other places, women were in general excluded in the Classic Age, when they could neither compete in nor even watch the events. Yet there were certain exceptions to this rule. First, as part of the accepted religious ritual at Olympia, a priestess of Demeter was actually expected to witness the contests and sat in a special seat with an excellent view. Also, though women could not participate directly in the events, they occasionally owned or sponsored the horses that competed in the horse and

Spectators cheer on the runners in the hoplitodromos *(race in armor), one of the events of the Olympic Games and other Greek athletic competitions. Women were barred from the Olympics.*

chariot races; and if their horses or teams won, they received the prizes and glory. Twice, for example, in 396 and 392 B.C., Kyniska, daughter of a Spartan king, won the Olympic chariot race. "My ancestors and my brothers were kings," she boasted. "I, Kyniska, won the chariot race with my swift-footed horses and erected this statue."[60] Several other Greek women won similar honors at Olympia and elsewhere.

A more singular exception occurred in 404 B.C. when a mother who wanted to watch her son compete in the Olympic boxing matches sneaked in disguised as a trainer. The ruse worked until the young man won. Then, unable to contain her excitement, the mother leaped over the barrier separating the trainers from the boxers, in the process revealing her gender. In deference to her son, father, and brothers, all of whom were Olympic winners, the judges allowed her to go unpunished. Supposedly, however, Olympic officials instituted a new rule stipulating that henceforth trainers, like athletes, had to attend the contests in the nude.

As a concession to women, many of whom evidently resented being excluded from competing in the Olympics, the people of Elis (the Peloponnesian state that sponsored the famous games) set up a small separate women's festival and games. Held at Olympia every four years, it was called the Heraea because it honored the goddess Hera (Zeus's wife). Sixteen Elean women organized and ran the games, which featured one event, a footrace of about 160 meters, with separate heats for different age groups. According to Pausanias,

> Every four years the sixteen women weave a robe for Hera, and the same women hold Hera's games. The games are a running match between virgin girls; they run with their hair let down

and their tunics rather above their knees, and the right breast and shoulder bared. The course for the race is the Olympic track, less about a sixth. They give the winners crowns made of olive-branches and a share of the ox they slaughter to Hera.[61]

Although women's participation in athletic competition was fairly limited in the Classic Age, by the end of that era times were changing rapidly. The Hellenistic Age would see a dramatic expansion of opportunities for women, not only in sports, but in many other areas as well.

5 Greek Women in Mythology, Drama, and Philosophy

Myths about goddesses and heroines, plays dramatizing their exploits and struggles, and the writings of Plato, Aristotle, and other philosophers are among the major surviving written sources that refer to ancient Greek women. Yet it is unclear how much the female characters in plays written in the Classic Age reflect real women, their personal views, and their real-life situations and problems.

In examining these sources, one is forced to conclude that they contain a varied and sometimes perplexing mixture of both real and unreal, both mundane and ideal characters and situations. On the one hand, the goddesses and sorceresses, with their superhuman and magical powers, are clearly unreal and/or ideal characters. And female characters in drama who defy the established order and either go on murderous rampages (such as Clytemnestra and Medea) or die upholding a noble ideal (Antigone) are more archetypes (exaggerated or ideal human examples or models) than real flesh-and-blood women. Similarly, the women Plato envisions in his *Republic* are members of an ideal, utopian society. He and other Greek philosophers often described women the way they and other men thought they

should or could be; or else they repeated the traditional view that women were inferior in one way or another. Indeed, in these works, as in those of the great playwrights, images of women were shaped, to one degree or another, by the prejudices and stereotypes of a staunchly male-dominated society.

On the other hand, the settings of the Greek myths, plays, and philosophical works are usually the real world; so they cannot help but reflect, to some extent, real social customs, situations, conventions, and characters. Numerous such examples can be found in the works of Euripides (ca. 485–406 B.C.), one of the three masters (along with Aeschylus and Sophocles) of fifth-century B.C. Athenian tragedy. "In subtle ways," says Sarah B. Pomeroy,

> Euripides reveals an intimacy with women's daily lives remarkable among classical Greek authors. He knows that upon returning from a party a husband quickly falls asleep, but that the wife needs time to prepare for bed. . . . [He] recognizes that childbirth is a painful ordeal, that daughters are best helped by their

CONSTRUCTIVE AND DESTRUCTIVE FEMALE BEINGS

In Greek mythology, goddesses, mortal women, and various female beings and creatures were usually portrayed in a black-and-white, "either-or" manner. That is, they were either virginal, helpful, virtuous, and/or constructive, or they were sexually active, devious, evil, and/or destructive. The Muses and Graces were among the constructive beings. Nine daughters born of Zeus and the goddess Memory, the Muses were thought to inspire humans with creative ability in the arts, music, and intellectual pursuits; the three Graces, who were also daughters of Zeus, personified grace and beauty and enhanced life's enjoyment.

In contrast, the Greek myths were more heavily populated with destructive beings. The Harpies, for example, disgusting creatures with birds' bodies and women's faces, were best known for stealing human food or else rendering it inedible. And the city of Thebes was supposedly terrorized by the Sphinx, a fearsome monster with a woman's head and a lion's body, who devoured numerous people. The Gorgons were female monsters, too. They had snakes for hair, and one of them, Medusa, was so hideous that anyone who looked at her turned to stone. In addition, there were the fearsome Furies, spirits of vengeance who relentlessly chased down and punished murderers and other transgressors. Following the "either-or" pattern, the goddess Athena eventually transformed the Furies into the Eumenides, which were kindly and beneficent spirits.

This head of the Gorgon Medusa was carved by the seventeenth-century Italian master Giovanni Bernini.

mothers on these occasions, and that after giving birth women are disheveled and haggard. Although the dramatic date is the Bronze Age, the . . . questions of female etiquette in Euripidean tragedy anachronistically agree with the conventions of classical Athens: women, especially unmarried ones, should remain indoors; they should not adorn themselves nor go outdoors when their husbands are away, nor should they converse with men in public; out of doors a woman should wear a veil; she should not look at a man in the face, not even her husband.[62]

Scholars often single out Euripides in this respect because his works often questioned traditional religious and social values and portrayed humans in a more realistic than heroic (larger-than-life) manner. (Hence, he has frequently been called the first playwright to deal with human problems in a modern way.) Yet even if Aeschylus and Sophocles more often pictured women in heroic, less than real ways, flashes of reality occasionally surface from their works. Consider, for example, this fragment from Sophocles' lost play, *Tereus*, the penetrating, plaintive lament of a real person:

Euripides, who often addressed women's problems in his plays, is depicted here holding the mask of tragedy in this Roman copy of a famous fourth-century B.C. Greek statue.

Often I pondered the status of women: we are nothing. As small girls in our father's house, we live the most delightful life, because ignorance keeps children happy. But when we come to the age of maturity and awareness, we are thrust out and bartered away, far from the gods of our forefathers and parents, some to alien men, some to barbarians, some to good homes and some to abusive ones. And after one single joyful night of love, we are compelled to praise this arrangement and consider ourselves lucky.[63]

Greek Goddesses as Female Role Models

It is instructive, therefore, to examine some of the best-known portrayals of women in Greek myths, plays, and philosophical writings and attempt to distinguish the real from the unreal. The obvious starting point is the way the Greeks envisioned their goddesses because these were the oldest, most traditional representations of women. In that strongly patriarchal society, of course, mythical personalities were shaped, either through oral transmission or in literature, largely by men, who tended to pigeonhole women in set roles. And just as Greek men cited the story of Pandora and the Amazon myths to exemplify women's flaws or unacceptable behavior, so too they pointed to various goddesses as positive or negative role models. It is hardly surprising, therefore, that these deities emerged as stereotypical, archetypal females with what might be described as "either-or" attributes and roles.

The "either" or the "or" depended to a considerable degree on a goddess's sexuality, an area Greek men went to great pains to regulate in their own wives and daughters. Either she was a virgin, a condition viewed as safe, or she was sexually active, which under certain circumstances could lead to undesirable outcomes. Goddesses like Athena, Artemis, and Hestia (protector of the hearth) for instance, were virgins and were most often portrayed as helpful and reliable; Hera and Aphrodite were sexually active and were frequently (though not always) pictured as hostile or dangerous, especially to men.

Athena certainly exemplified a positive female role model, at least from the point of view of Greek men. This was because, though she was portrayed as a strong-willed, powerful, and accomplished woman, she also helped to support and perpetuate the Greek patriarchal system. According to myth, she was not

The so-called "Mourning Athena," a relief that now rests in the Acropolis Museum. Ancient Greek men saw Athena as a positive role model for themselves.

born of a mother but instead sprang (fully clad in armor!) from Zeus's head. As Sue Blundell suggests, by using this mode of reproduction,

> [Zeus] ensures that no son will ever succeed to his position. Instead of a threatening male child, he begets a loyal daughter whose perpetual virginity is a guarantee of her refusal to be the source of any further challenge to his power. This does not mean that Zeus will never father children by the normal method (far from it). . . . It is in its tremendous potency as a symbol that the miraculous birth of Athena is significant. It sets the tone for the system of rule which it has helped to bring into being. This will be a system in which the male is utterly dominant, since even the female's role in reproduction can be dispensed with if Zeus puts his mind to it.[64]

Athena was also a positive role model because she was seen as highly disciplined and as an efficient manager, qualities considered desirable for a respectable Greek mother and housekeeper. But more importantly, her virginity was the model for the virgin status expected of a Greek bride; to a Greek man, it was important to marry a virgin to be absolutely sure that the children were his.

In contrast, the love goddess Aphrodite was often portrayed as promiscuous and adulterous. She, like Athena, had no mother. But Aphrodite's birth had a sexual, rather than asexual, dimension; namely, she rose miraculously from some white foam (*aphros*) produced when the

The adulterous goddess Aphrodite cavorts with Pan, god of shepherds, and Eros (the Roman Cupid), her frequent companion, in this sculpture dated to around 100 B.C.

sky god Uranus's genitals (which his son had cut off) fell into the sea. Subsequently, she was beautiful, friendly, and charming. But she also cheated on her husband, Hephaestos, god of the forge, by having affairs with Hermes, the messenger god, and Ares, the god of war.

Equally bad, Aphrodite frequently inspired lustful or adulterous desires in others, including married women, which sometimes led to tragedy. In the myth of Hippolytus (dramatized by Euripides in

429 B.C.), for example, the title character, the admirable son of the Athenian hero Theseus, scorned Aphrodite and worshiped Artemis instead. In retaliation, Aphrodite made Hippolytus's stepmother, Phaedra, fall in love with the youth in her husband's absence. Hippolytus honorably rejected her advances, but the humiliated Phaedra hanged herself. The returning Theseus, mistakenly believing that his wife and son had had an affair, cursed and banished the young man, who died soon afterward. That Aphrodite could come between father and son and/or husband and wife disturbed Greek men and made her a negative role model for respectable women.

It should be emphasized, again, that this negative view of Aphrodite was a male one. Thanks to some of Sappho's surviving verses, we know that at least some women pictured her more positively, as a nonthreatening, supporting, and reassuring influence. "Come here to me now," Sappho pleads of the goddess,

> free me from this aching pain, fulfill everything that my heart desires to be fulfilled; you, yes you, will be my ally. Leave Crete and come to me here [to Lesbos], to this temple [dedicated to the goddess], where the loveliness of your apple grove waits for you. . . . There, a meadow, a pasture for horses, blooms with all the flowers of Spring, while the breezes flow gently.[65]

It is unfortunate that so few such personal expressions by Greek women have survived; for Greek men's stereotypical depictions of female divinities reveal almost nothing about how real women thought and felt.

DRAMA'S LARGER-THAN-LIFE WOMEN

Compensating somewhat for this oversight were the often complex and sometimes sympathetic depictions of women in the plays of the great dramatists. For a gender so often segregated, regulated, and denied numerous political and other rights, women assumed a stature of surprising importance in Greek tragedy. Of Aeschylus's seven complete surviving plays, Sophocles' seven, and Euripides' nineteen, woman have central or at least prominent roles in most; and the titles of over half of these thirty-three works consist of the names of either individual women (e.g., *Medea, Helen*) or groups of women *(The Trojan Women, The Suppliant Women)*. Moreover, the plots of many of these plays revolve around conflicts between men and women or women and society.

As the lament from Sophocles' *Tereus* illustrates, he and his colleagues (including the comic playwright Aristophanes) could at times create female characters who spoke and/or acted like real women. But this was usually for only part of the time that they were on stage. (It should be noted that women were not allowed on stage; the accepted convention was for men to play women's parts.) Overall, though the major female characters in the these plays express human emotions magnificently, they

ANTIGONE MEDDLES IN MEN'S AFFAIRS

In this excerpt from her book Women in Ancient Greece, *noted scholar Sue Blundell explains how Antigone, the title character of one of Sophocles' most famous plays, was a "boundary crosser" who meddled in men's affairs.*

"In Sophocles' tragedy *Antigone,* the heroine rebels against the law of the state by attempting to perform funeral rites for her dead brother, who in a decree introduced by her uncle, King Creon, has been refused burial on the grounds that he was a traitor. Antigone's sister Ismene pleads with her not to overstep the normal bounds of female behavior: 'Remember we are women. . . . We're not born to contend with men'; and Creon, justifying his refusal to pardon Antigone, urges that 'we must defend the men who live by law . . . [and] never let some woman triumph over us.' Although Antigone is engaged in traditional areas of female activity—mourning the dead, defending the interests of the family—she is asserting herself in a masculine fashion in order to do so. At the same time Creon feels that his own manhood is being threatened: 'I am not the man, not now. She is the man . . . if this victory goes to her and she goes free.' Both parties come to grief. Antigone is condemned to . . . [be] walled up in an underground vault—and hangs herself. Creon's son, Haemon, Antigone's betrothed, and Creon's wife Eurydice both commit suicide."

A modern rendering of Antigone, heroine of Sophocles' play of the same name, and her sister, Ismene.

often do so in a magnified, larger-than-life manner. Greek play production was visually, verbally, and emotionally stylized rather than realistic (as opera, musical comedy, and vampire films are today). So in shaping both male and female characters, the playwrights regularly depicted them in idealized or extreme situations of good or evil, either to make a moral statement or to entertain.

One common and effective way the dramatists used female characters to make statements about society, life, fate, and so on was to give them traditionally masculine attributes and roles. Aristophanes' farcical *Lysistrata,* written in 411 B.C., when the Peloponnesian War had already devas-

The comic playwright Aristophanes, depicted here, blurred the boundary between female and male social roles in plays such as Lysistrata *and* Women in the Assembly.

tated Greece for twenty years, is a prime example. The title character, whose name means "She Who Disbands Armies," organizes the Athenian women, who seize control of the Acropolis and the city's treasury. This act, coupled with their refusal to have sex with their husbands, forces the men to make peace with Sparta and end the war. By having them interfere in war, policy making, and other male spheres, Aristophanes makes the women "boundary crossers." The audacity and absurdity of their assuming male roles and managing to make peace helps to hammer home the playwright's main point—that Greek men have so far failed to end the war. Aristophanes also employed such boundary-crossing roles in his *Women in the Assembly* (ca. 392 B.C.). In the play, a group of women disguised as men sneak into the all-male legislature and manage to get a bill passed that transfers political power to the city's women.

Tragedy, too, featured women assuming male roles. In Aeschylus's *Agamemnon* (458 B.C.), for example, the title character's wife, Clytemnestra, chooses her own sexual partner (Agamemnon's cousin) and rules the kingdom while her husband is away fighting at Troy. And when he returns, she kills him. The playwright's audience undoubtedly identified all of these acts as typically masculine. And it made a similar judgment about the title character of Euripides' *Medea* (431 B.C.). Just before going on a bloody killing spree (including her own children), Medea utters these words, which sound eerily like those of a male hero going off to war: "Let no one think of me as humble or weak or passive [all traditional female traits]; let them understand I am of a different kind: dangerous to my enemies, loyal to my friends. To such a life glory belongs."[66]

MISOGYNY OR SYMPATHY?

Drama was also a medium in which the male playwrights could publicly express their feelings about women and/or force their audiences to think about women and women's issues. Some of the character traits and deeds of their female characters—the boundary crossing and the homicidal fury of Clytemnestra and Medea, for instance—were uncomplimentary; these tended to reinforce traditional negative stereotypes of women and perpetuate misogyny. Another vivid example is this bitter speech made by the title character of Euripides' *Hippolytus* after learning of his stepmother's desire for him:

> O Zeus, why did you house them in the light of day, women, man's evil, a false glittering counterfeit? . . . This makes it clear how great an evil woman is. The father who breeds and educates one pays a dowry too that she may live elsewhere and he be free from pain. And then the man who takes this curse inside his house delights in adding fine adornments to her shape . . . spends time in finding dresses for her, the fool, and wastes away the substance of his house. . . . Easiest for him who has settled in his home a wife whose mind's a total blank, a simple useless thing. I hate a clever woman, and . . . I would de-

A nineteenth-century depiction of Euripides' tragic heroine Medea, who kills her own children to get revenge on her husband who abandoned her.

stroy you all. Never shall I have enough of hating women.[67]

Yet at times the dramatists were just as emphatically sympathetic to women and the plight of their social repression. Perhaps the most famous example is this speech by Euripides' Medea:

> Surely, of all the creatures that have life and will, we women are the most wretched. When, for an extravagant sum [i.e., the dowry], we have bought a husband, we must then accept him as professor of our body. . . . Will the

man we get be bad or good? For women, divorce is not respectable; to repel the man, not possible. . . . If a man grows tired of the company at home, he can go out, and find a cure for tediousness. We wives are forced to look to one man only. And, they tell us, we at home live free from danger, they go out to battle. Fools! I'd rather stand three times in the front line [in battle] than bear one child.[68]

On the surface, it may seem incredible that the same person wrote both of these speeches, one so critical of women, the other so sympathetic. But in fact, the issues of women's abilities and rights were being debated in various ways in Athens in Euripides' time; and these and other similar excerpts from his plays suggest that he may have been attempting to present both sides of the debate. In this view, the playwright did not intend for "his audience simply to accept the misogynistic maxims," as Pomeroy puts it.

> Rather, he uses the extreme vantage point of misogyny as a means of examining popular beliefs about women. . . . Euripides counters the idea expressed in the misogynistic platitudes by portraying individual women and their reasons for their actions. . . . [For example,] the double standard of sexual morality is implicit in many of the myths Euripides chose as the basis of his plots. He is the first author we know of to look at this topic from both the woman's and the man's point of view. . . . Euripides does not advocate that women should have the same sex-

ual freedom as men, but rather suggests that it is better for all concerned if the husband is as monogamous as the wife.[69]

The fact that Euripides often challenged the men in his audiences to reexamine their treatment of women was surely one of the reasons that he was far less popular than the other great tragedians in his own time.

PLATO AND ARISTOTLE ON WOMEN

In the century following the first performances of the works of the great dramatists, the philosophers Plato and Aristotle also expressed their views about women and came to some differing conclusions. A few scholars have called Plato the world's first feminist, or advocate of women's rights. They base this on some of the radical proposals for reordering society he made in his masterpiece the *Republic*. In the ideal state/society he envisions, the highest social class will consist of rulers and soldiers—the Guardians—and women will be admitted to this elite group along with men. Because "women are to have the same duties as men, they must have the same nurture and education," he concludes. "Women must be taught music and gymnastics and also the art of war, which they must practice like the men," for

> there is no special faculty of administration in a state which a woman has because she is a woman, or which a man has by virtue of his sex, but the

gifts of nature are diffused in both. . . . One woman has a gift of healing, another not; one is a musician and another has no music in her nature. . . . And one woman is a philosopher, and another is an enemy of philosophy. . . . [It follows then that] one woman will have the temper of a Guardian, and another not. Was not the selection of the male Guardians determined by differences of this sort? . . . Men and women alike possess the qualities which make a Guardian; they differ only in their comparative strengths and weaknesses.[70]

At first glance, Plato's utopia sounds very promising for Greek women. Yet though his ideas about women ruling and fighting alongside men were certainly radical and progressive for his time and place, he did not believe or advocate that women were men's true equals. He also explains in the *Republic* that only a very few women can be expected to qualify for Guardian status. This is because on the whole women are weaker and less talented than men, in a way "imperfect men." Moreover, in a later utopian work, the *Laws*, he modified his stance on women, assigning them somewhat more traditional traits, such as obedience and modesty. He also warned that they could be devious and criticized the freedoms allowed Spartan women, a policy he felt had weakened Sparta's social fabric.

Plato (left) and Aristotle walk together in this detail from The School of Athens, *a magnificent fresco completed in 1511 by the Italian master Raphael (Raffaello Sanzio, 1483–1520).*

WOMEN PRONE TO SECRECY AND STEALTH?

In his Laws *(Benjamin Jowett's translation), Plato portrays an Athenian speaking with a Spartan and a Cretan. In Sparta, most of the men ate their meals with their male comrades in a common mess hall; and the Athenian criticizes the lack of "public tables" for Spartan women, in the process revealing some of Plato's misgivings about women.*

"You are mistaken in leaving the women unregulated by law. . . . That part of the human race which is by nature prone to secrecy and stealth on account of their weakness—I mean the female sex—has been left without regulation [in Sparta], which is a great mistake. . . . For the neglect of regulations about women may not only be regarded as a neglect of half the entire matter, but in proportion as women's nature is inferior to that of men in capacity for virtue, in that degree the consequence of such neglect is more than twice as important. . . . At present, such is the unfortunate condition of mankind, that no man of sense will even venture to speak of common tables in cities in which they have never been established at all; and how can anyone avoid being utterly ridiculous, who attempts to compel women to show in public how much they eat and drink? There is nothing at which the [female] sex is more likely to take offense. For women are accustomed to creep into dark places, and when dragged out into the light they will exert their utmost powers of resistance."

Because he failed to embrace the idea of complete male-female equality, Plato was not a true feminist. Yet at least he was willing to admit that some women were smarter and worthier than some men, and, in principle, he supported the notion of equal opportunity for women. For these reasons, scholar Michael Grant's appraisal—that Plato was "the nearest approach to a systematic feminist produced by the Greco-Roman world"[71]—seems a fair one.

By contrast, Plato's most famous pupil, Aristotle, consistently presented philosophical arguments supporting traditional views of women as "naturally" inferior and subordinate to men. To his credit, Aristotle did advocate better education for women; however, this was to improve the quality of their traditional household duties rather than to afford them expanded social and political opportunities. Mincing no words, he states in his *Politics,*

The male is by nature superior, and the female inferior; and one rules, and the other is ruled; this principle, of necessity, extends to all mankind. . . . The male is by nature fitter for command than the female, just as the older and full-grown is superior to the younger and more immature. . . . The courage and justice of a man and of a woman are not, as Socrates maintained, the same; the courage of a man is shown in commanding, of a woman in obeying.[72]

Furthermore, says Aristotle, women are morally inferior to men, men are "spirit" while women are merely "matter," marriages are friendships between unequals, and when women are allowed too many rights and privileges, society suffers, as in the notorious case of Sparta.

Aristotle was a brilliant scholar, and many of his scientific writings were based on logic and creative thinking and established new ways of thinking about certain aspects of the natural world. On the subject of women's roles and rights, however, he seemed content to fall back on custom and tradition and to perpetuate the patriarchal status quo. Indeed, with the notable exceptions of some of Euripides' characters and speeches and Plato's female Guardians, the Greek myths, plays, and philosophical tracts are heavily biased by the traditional male perspective. Some facts about real women's status, rights, duties, and habits do emerge from these sources. But their general lack of a true female point of view, along with their tendency to depict or talk about ideal rather than real women, compels us to examine them with caution.

Chapter

6 The Lives of Greek Women Improve in the Hellenistic Age

During the last historical period in which the ancient Greek city-states and kingdoms enjoyed self-rule—the Hellenistic Age—Greek women experienced marked improvements in their legal and social status and economic opportunities. The word *Hellenistic* means "Greek-like" and refers to the overlay of Greek language, customs,

The Apollo Belvedere, *a Roman copy of a Greek original created around 330 B.C. The popular god was the divine inspirer of poetry and music, which flourished in Hellenistic times.*

82 ■ WOMEN OF ANCIENT GREECE

and ideas onto the cultures of the Near East in the three centuries following the death of the famous Macedonian Greek ruler Alexander the Great in 323 B.C. In just ten years Alexander conquered the vast Persian Empire (centered in what are now Iran and Iraq), in the process spreading Greek language, political administration, and culture to many parts of the Near East. But the huge kingdom that he had created was immediately torn asunder as his leading generals and governors faced off and came to death grips. For the next forty-odd years, these bitter rivals, who came to be called "the Successors," waged almost unrelenting war. Finally, by about 280 B.C., three major new Greek realms had emerged: the Ptolemaic Kingdom (made up mainly of Egypt), the Seleucid Kingdom (spanning the heart of the old Persian Empire and parts of Asia Minor), and the Macedonian Kingdom (encompassing Macedonia and much of Greece).

The Hellenistic period witnessed widespread experimentation, new horizons, and notable achievement in the arts, sciences, and numerous social institutions. A spirit of searching for the underlying truth of things found expression in the arts, as poets, sculptors, and painters achieved levels of vividness and realism unknown in prior ages. The new spirit also created "a greatly enhanced interest in the individual human being and his mind and emotions," says Michael Grant,

an interest given vigorous expression by biographers and portrait artists. And this concern for the individual was extended not only to men but to women, whose position in society, literature and art underwent an unprecedented transformation that was one of the most remarkable evolutionary changes of the age.[73]

The reasons for this transformation of women's position are not completely clear. But the decline of the independent city-state, with its local institutions closely protecting and regulating women, and the simultaneous emergence of absolute monarchies were surely factors. In the large Greek kingdoms, in which the kings made the laws, most men possessed fewer political rights and privileges than they had in the more democratic *polis* system. As a result, Sarah B. Pomeroy points out, "on the one hand, the gap in privileges between men and women was much narrowed, and on the other, the men—rather than attempting to hoard them—became more ready to share with women the less-valued privileges they had."[74] (It must be emphasized that not all Hellenistic women experienced the same degree of liberation since both regional and class differences came into play. For example, improvements in Athenian women's lives appear to have been minimal as compared to those of their Ptolemaic and Macedonian counterparts. Likewise, poorer women continued to have fewer opportunities than well-to-do ones.[75])

THE HELLENISTIC QUEENS

Another important factor in the improved status of women was the rise of the Hellenistic queen as a political and social

DELPHI HEAPS HONORS ON A WOMAN

This translation of an inscription from Delphi, home of the famous religious oracle, records the honors that the city bestowed on a female musician named Polygnota in 86 B.C. (late Hellenistic times). In prior ages, only men received and exercised most of these privileges. (This excerpt is from Lefkowitz's and Fant's sourcebook).

"The city of Delphi has decreed: whereas Polygnota, daughter of Socrates [not the philosopher], a Theban harpist having come to Delphi, at the appointed time of the Pythian games . . . began on that very day and gave a day's time and performed at the request of the archons [local administrators] and citizens for three days, and won the highest degree of respect, deserving the praise of Apollo and of the Theban people and of our city—she is awarded a crown and 500 drachmas. With good fortune. Voted: to commend Polygnota . . . for her piety and reverence towards the god and for her dedication to her profession; to bestow on her and her descendants the guest-friendship of the city, the right to consult the oracle, the privileges of being heard first, of safety, of exemption from taxes, and of front seating at the games held by the city, the right of owning land and a house and all the other honors ordinarily awarded to other benefactors of the city; to invite her to the town hall to the public hearth, and provide her with a victim [animal] to sacrifice to Apollo. To the god. With good fortune."

phenomenon. A number of royal women in this era, especially in Ptolemaic Egypt, achieved considerable political independence and power; over time, this likely translated into social influence as these gains, in Grant's words, "percolated down the social scale, so that ordinary Hellenistic women, too, became much freer."[76]

The models for the queens of the era following Alexander were his grandmother, Eurydice, and mother, Olympias. Like him, both were ambitious, ruthless, and shrewd; and both owned their own lands and ad-

ministered considerable wealth without the guidance of men. Furthermore, when Alexander was away conquering Persia, though Olympias was not sole ruler of Macedonia (technically Alexander's regent, Antipater, was in charge), she exercised a good deal of power. One of the Successors murdered her a few years after her son's death, but other Macedonian queens soon followed the example she had set—that of a strong female authority figure.

One of the greatest of these queens was Arsinoë (ar-SIN-oh-eh) II, wife and sister of the second Ptolemaic king, Ptolemy II Philadelphus, who reigned from 283 to 246 B.C. (The Ptolemies adopted certain Egyptian royal customs, including marriage between siblings.) A talented, energetic woman, she apparently exerted a strong influence on her husband, perhaps even in political and military matters (although the story that she helped him plan the deployment of his war fleets is likely exaggerated). Arsinoë was also a patron of literature and architecture and had some superb sculptures made of herself, which contributed to the ongoing emergence of realistic female portraiture. She was also deified (proclaimed a god), along with her husband, while still living. Grant aptly calls her "a forerunner of the Roman empress of the future."[77]

Among the other prominent and at times powerful Hellenistic queens was Berenice II (mother of Ptolemy IV), who led a successful rebellion in 247 B.C., seizing the Egyptian throne and ruling briefly with her son. Later, in the 190s B.C., Cleopatra I ruled Egypt essentially alone, as regent for her own son (Ptolemy VI). And another Ptolemy, Cleopatra Thea (died 121 B.C.), who married three different Seleucid kings and mothered two more, was long a powerful force behind the scenes in the Seleucid court. The fact that she was the only Seleucid queen who minted coins on which her portrait appeared alone, illustrates that she achieved uncommon stature for a woman.

By far the best known of all the Hellenistic queens, and perhaps the most famous woman leader of all times, was also a Ptolemy. Cleopatra VII (69–30 B.C.), the

This coin was minted by Cleopatra VII, the renowned Hellenistic Greek queen of Egypt who joined forces with Rome's Mark Antony.

daughter of weak king Ptolemy XII, secured the Egyptian throne with the aid of the powerful Roman statesman-general Julius Caesar. By the first century B.C., the Macedonian and Seleucid kingdoms had already been largely absorbed by Rome, and the Ptolemaic realm had been reduced to a pawn in the power struggles of the leading Romans of the day. But the enormously ambitious, bold, and talented Cleopatra shrewdly played the international power game as well as or better than most of these men. After Caesar's assassination in 44 B.C., she ruled Egypt alone and quite effectively for several years. Eventually, she became the lover and ally of another powerful Roman, Mark Antony; together, hoping to create an empire encompassing the remnants of Alexander's old realm and more, they challenged the might of Rome. But Antony's chief rival, Octavian (later Augustus, the first Roman emperor), decisively defeated them at Actium in western Greece in 31 B.C. The lovers committed suicide soon afterward, bringing the Hellenistic Age, the last ancient period of Greek autonomy, to a close.

INCREASED ECONOMIC AND LEGAL RIGHTS

Although Arsinoë, Cleopatra, and some of the other queens were the only Hellenistic Greek women to wield such extensive power and influence, on the local level several others held honorary citizenship and on occasion even political office. In 218 B.C. the people of Lamia (in central Greece) granted honorary citizenship to Aristodama, a poetess from Smyrna (on the coast of Asia Minor), for example. This was evidently in recognition of her praise for the Lamians and their ancestors in her works. And a female *archon* (administrator) is mentioned in a second-century B.C. inscription from Histria, a Greek town in what is now Romania. Another woman magistrate, Phile, from Priene (in western Asia Minor), earned fame for overseeing the construction of an aqueduct in the first century B.C.

Though these cases were probably exceptional and most women were still excluded from political life, large numbers of Hellenistic women enjoyed expanded economic rights and clout. Documents written on papyrus, mostly discovered in Egypt, show that women in that region (both Greek and native Egyptian) regularly gave and received loans; bought and sold land, slaves, and other property; inherited and bequeathed property and other legacies; and even made their own

---

AN EPITAPH FOR AN ACTRESS

In Hellenistic times, society looked down on entertainers, whether male or female. This third-century B.C. funerary inscription (reproduced from Lefkowitz's and Fant's sourcebook) is dedicated to an actress, presumably by a friend.

"In the past she won resounding fame in many towns and many cities for her various accomplishments in plays, mimes, and choruses, and (often) dances. But she did not die on the stage, this tenth Muse. To Bassilla the actress, Heracleides, the skilled speaker and biographer, set up this stone. Even though she is dead, she will have the same honor she had in life, when she made her body 'die' on the floor of the stage. This is what her fellow actors are saying to her: 'Bassilla farewell, no one lives forever.'"

marriage contracts, perhaps sometimes without the consent of their fathers or other guardians. (In Sparta, meanwhile, female landowners continued to be plentiful, some of them attaining great wealth.) One surviving marriage contract from Greek-ruled Egypt—that of newlyweds named Heraclides and Demetria, dated 311 B.C.—reveals not only some of the bride's apparently considerable legal rights but also that the groom was obligated to respect them:

> Heraclides takes as his lawful wife Demetria of Cos. . . . He is free; she is free. She brings with her to the marriage clothing and ornaments valued at 1000 drachmas [a considerable sum]. Heraclides shall supply to Demetria all that is suitable for a freeborn wife. . . . If Demetria is caught in fraudulent machinations [actions] to the disgrace of her husband Heraclides, she shall forfeit all she has brought with her. But Heraclides shall prove whatever he charges against Demetria before three men whom they both approve. It shall not be lawful for Heraclides to bring home another woman for himself . . . nor to have children by another woman, nor to indulge in fraudulent machinations against Demetria on any pretext. If Heraclides is caught doing any of these things, and Demetria proves it before three men whom they both approve, Heraclides shall return to Demetria the dowry of 1000 drachmas which she has brought, and also forfeit 1000 drachmas [of his own money]. . . . Demetria shall have the right to exact payment from Heraclides and from his property on both land and sea, as if by a legal judgment. . . . Heraclides and Demetria shall each have the right to keep a copy of the contract in their own custody, and to produce it against one another.[78]

The differences between this marriage and an average Athenian one from the same period are striking. Heraclides could not bring home or have children by a concubine whereas an Athenian man could do both. And both Heraclides and Demetria had equal recourse to seek legal and financial damages in case the other did not honor the contract. Such a legal arrangement was unheard-of in Athens in the late fourth century B.C. (In fact, during this period, as the treatment of women in other Greek areas was becoming more liberal, the Athenian government actually restricted women more than before.)

LITERATURE CAPTURES THE NEW FREEDOM

These advances in women's rights were accompanied in many places by corresponding increases in their personal freedom. Passages from Hellenistic poems, plays, and other writings suggest that women were less segregated than before and in some areas could walk around the streets without a male escort.

Even in Athens, where women's lives were still unusually restricted in Hellenistic times, some women were less afraid to stand up to their fathers and other male

This figurine of a Hellenistic woman holding a fan captures a common women's dress style and hairstyle of that unusually liberal era.

between man and wife; he must love her, always, until the end, and she must never cease to do what gives her husband pleasure. He was all that I wished with regard to me, and my pleasure is his pleasure. But suppose he is satisfactory as far as I am concerned but is bankrupt, and you . . . now want to give me to a rich man to save me from living out my life in distress. Where does so much money exist, father, that having it can give me more pleasure than my husband can? How can it be just or honorable that I should take a share of any good things he has, but take no share in his poverty? . . . When I was a young girl, you had to find a husband [for] me, when the choice was yours. But once you had given me to a husband, from that moment this responsibility belonged to me, naturally, because if I make a mistake in judgment, it's my own life that I shall ruin.[79]

Hellenistic literature (and art, too) also tended to depict romantic love and passion between men and women. By contrast with literary and artistic depictions from prior ages, in which women were typically either chaste mothers or men's sex objects, the new age emphasized men and women as sexual equals, genuinely interested in each other's needs and pleasures. The most conspicuous literary example is the *Argonautica (Voyage of the Argo)*, an epic poem about the mythical search for the Golden Fleece, by Apollonius of Rhodes (ca. 295–215 B.C.). The passion felt for the hero, Jason, by the

authorities. In the following fragment from an anonymous comic play, an Athenian maid boldly asserts herself when her father tries to dissolve her marriage and force her to marry a richer man:

> Father, you ought to be making the speech that I am now making, because you ought to have more sense than I have. . . . There is a covenant

heroine, Medea, is captured in this smoldering passage:

> She reveled in his need of her and would have poured out all her soul to him as well, so captivating was the light of love that streamed from Jason's golden head and held her gleaming eyes. Her heart was warmed and melted like the dew on roses under the morning sun.[80]

A NUMBER OF ACCOMPLISHED WOMEN

Hellenistic women were not only the subjects of literature and art but also, in some cases, accomplished writers and artists in their own right. This was possible in part because educational opportunities for women in many parts of the Greek world increased during this

This highly fanciful and romanticized rendering of Jason and Medea, from Apollonius's Argonautica, *is by the French painter Gustave Moreau (1826–1898).*

period. On the one hand, barriers against female physical education and athletic competition steadily eroded. The more liberated women of these times demanded that they be allowed to watch and participate in more than just the female-only Heraea. And by the first century B.C., the Pythian, Isthmian, and Nemean games, along with many local games, both admitted women as spectators and allowed them to compete in several events (although probably only against other women).

On the other hand, more women became literate than ever before, and there is evidence that in some areas girls attended formal schools along with boys. This trend produced a number of female poets and even a few women painters, sculptors, and philosophers. Information about most of these individuals is scarce, and most of their works have not survived. But we do have some short poems and fragments by Erinna of Telos (late fourth century B.C.), Anyte of Tegea (third century B.C.), Nossis of Locri (third century B.C.), and others.

HELLENISTIC POETS

These epigrams (short poems expressing single thoughts or observations) by the Hellenistic women writers Anyte of Tegea and Nossis of Locri are excerpted from Lefkowitz's and Fant's sourcebook.

Anyte

"I weep for Antibia, a virgin. Many suitors wanted her and came to her father's house, because she was known for her beauty and cleverness. But deadly Fate sent all their hopes rolling away."

"Often here on her daughter's tomb, Cleina in her sorrow cried for her dear child who died too soon, calling back Philaenis's soul. Before she could be married, she crossed the pale stream of Acheron [a river in the underworld]."

Nossis

"This picture captures Thaumarete's form—how well he [the artist] painted her pride and her beauty, her gentle eyes. If your little watch-dog saw you, she would wag her tail, and think that she saw the mistress of her house."

"This picture—the image she made of herself, Callo set here in blonde Aphrodite's house [temple]. How gently she stands there. Her charm blooms. I greet her. There is no blemish at all in her life."

The massive and magnificent Nike *(Victory) of* Samothrace, *carved by an unknown Rhodian sculptor, captures the creative, highly expressive spirit of the Hellenistic Age when many Greek women achieved various degrees of social liberation.*

There are also a number of surviving references to the controversial female philosopher Hipparchia. She was the disciple and wife of Crates of Thebes, a member of the Cynic philosophical movement. The Cynics, founded by the radical thinker Antisthenes in the fourth century B.C., held that happiness derives from virtue rather than from luxury and material pleasures; thus, people should lead austere, self-disciplined lives. They also believed that men and women are equally

virtuous and advocated complete women's liberation. Concerning Hipparchia's life and intellectual capabilities, the third-century A.D. Greek biographer Diogenes Laertius recorded that she

fell in love with the discourses and the life of Crates, and would not pay attention to any of her suitors, their wealth, their high birth, or their beauty. But to her Crates was everything. . . . Adopting the same dress, [she] went about with her husband

and lived with him in public and went out to dinners with him. Accordingly, she appeared at the banquet given by Lysimachus, and there put down Theodorus, known as the Atheist, by means of the following trick. Any action which would not be called wrong if done by Theodorus, would not be called wrong if done by Hipparchia. Now Theodorus does no wrong when he strikes himself; therefore neither does Hipparchia do wrong when she strikes Theodorus. He had no reply with which to meet the argument.[81]

Hipparchia was no average woman, even in the more liberal Hellenistic period.

Yet the social and cultural currents of that era allowed many, if not most, Greek women more freedom and opportunity than they had ever known. All through the age, times were clearly changing for women, as they were for everyone in the Greek world, in large part because Rome conquered and absorbed that world by the end of the first century B.C. The former Greek lands became Roman provinces, and over time the lives of most Greek and Roman women in a sense merged in the larger melting pot of the vast Roman Empire. But the story of Roman women, which is as intricate and fascinating as that of their Greek sisters, must be told elsewhere.

Notes

Introduction: A Limited but Tantalizing Picture of Greek Women

1. Sarah B. Pomeroy, *Goddesses, Whores, Wives, and Slaves: Women in Classical Antiquity.* New York: Shocken Books, 1975, p. xv.

Chapter 1: Women in Early Greek Societies

2. Eva Cantarella, *Pandora's Daughters: The Role and Status of Women in Greek and Roman Antiquity,* trans. Maureen B. Fant. Baltimore: Johns Hopkins University Press, 1987, pp. 24–25.

3. Hesiod, *Theogony,* in *Hesiod and Theognis,* trans. Dorothea Wender. New York: Penguin Books, 1973, p. 42.

4. Semonides, *On Women,* in Mary R. Lefkowitz and Maureen B. Fant, eds., *Women's Life in Greece and Rome: A Source Book in Translation.* Baltimore: Johns Hopkins University Press, 1992, p. 27.

5. Semonides, *On Women,* in Lefkowitz and Fant, *Women's Life in Greece and Rome,* p. 27.

6. Homer, *Odyssey,* trans. E. V. Rieu. Baltimore: Penguin Books, 1961, p. 283.

7. Homer, *Iliad,* trans. Robert Fagles. New York: Penguin Books, 1990, p. 210.

8. Homer, *Iliad,* p. 211.

9. Sue Blundell, *Women in Ancient Greece.* Cambridge, MA: Harvard University Press, 1995, p. 62.

10. Pomeroy, *Goddesses, Whores, Wives, and Slaves,* p. 23.

11. Cantarella, *Pandora's Daughters,* pp. 15–16.

12. Homer, *Iliad,* p. 339.

13. Sappho, Fragment 75, in *Sappho: Poems and Fragments,* trans. Josephine Balmer. Secaucus, NJ: Meadowland Books, 1984, p. 76.

14. Blundell, *Women in Ancient Greece,* p. 67.

Chapter 2: Women's Legal Status and Rights in the Classic Age

15. Quoted in Lefkowitz and Fant, *Women's Life in Greece and Rome,* p. 59. This funeral law comes from an inscription found on the island of Keos (located a few miles southeast of Athens) and is thought to be a copy of Solon's law, the original version of which is lost.

16. She was unnamed because it was considered improper to mention a respectable woman's name in court or other public forums.

17. From Lysias, *Against Diogeiton,* quoted in Lefkowitz and Fant, *Women's Life in Greece and Rome,* p. 63. Note: Lysias was the speechwriter *(logographos)* hired by the son to compose the speech recited in court by the son-in-law.

18. Lysias, *Against Diogeiton,* quoted in Lefkowitz and Fant, *Women's Life in Greece and Rome,* p. 63.

19. Eva C. Keuls, *The Reign of the Phallus: Sexual Politics in Ancient Athens.* New York: Harper and Row, 1985, p. 104.

20. Pomeroy, *Goddesses, Whores, Wives, and Slaves,* p. 64.

21. Blundell, *Women in Ancient Greece,* pp. 122–23.

22. Blundell, *Women in Ancient Greece,* p. 68.

23. Female relatives, including sisters and aunts, also figured in the *anchisteia.* So in extremely rare cases in which any and all uncles, male cousins, and other male relatives were lacking, a female family member might inherit the property, at least in theory. It is doubtful, however, that this actually happened very often. See David M. Schaps, *The Economic Rights of Women in Ancient Greece.*

Edinburgh, Scotland: Edinburgh University Press, 1979, pp. 5–6.

24. Other common punishments for adulterers, though less severe, were seen as extremely humiliating. These included *paratilmos,* shaving the offender's pubic hair; and *rhaphanidosis,* shoving a large radish up the offender's anus.

25. The first-century A.D. Greek biographer and moralist Plutarch tells of the poetess Telesilla organizing the Argive women to defend their land in the late sixth century B.C. in his *Moralia* (quoted in Lefkowitz and Fant's *Women's Life in Greece and Rome,* pp. 129–30); and the second-century A.D. Greek traveler Pausanias relates a similar story about the women of Tegea in the seventh century B.C. in his *Guide to Greece* (quoted in *Women's Life in Greece and Rome,* p. 130).

26. Blundell, *Women in Ancient Greece,* p. 151.

27. Plutarch, *Sayings of Spartan Women,* in *Plutarch on Sparta,* trans. Richard J. A. Talbert. New York: Penguin Books, 1988, pp. 158–59.

28. Plutarch, *Life of Agis,* in *Plutarch on Sparta,* p. 58.

29. Plutarch, *Life of Agis,* in *Plutarch on Sparta,* pp. 56, 58.

Chapter 3: The Home Life of Classical Greek Women

30. Xenophon, *Oeconomicus,* in *Xenophon: Conversations of Socrates,* trans., Hugh Tredennick and Robin Waterfield. New York: Penguin Books, 1990, pp. 314–15.

31. Blundell, *Women in Ancient Greece,* p. 136–37.

32. Blundell, *Women in Ancient Greece,* p. 136–37.

33. Cornelius Nepos, *The Book of the Great Generals of Foreign Nations,* trans. John Rolfe. Cambridge, MA: Harvard University Press, 1960, p. 371.

34. Aristophanes, *Lysistrata,* in *The Complete Plays of Aristophanes,* trans. Moses Hadas. New York: Bantam Books, 1962, p. 289.

35. Xenophon, *Oeconomicus,* in *Conversations of Socrates,* pp. 315–17.

36. Quoted in Lefkowitz and Fant, *Women's Life in Greece and Rome,* p. 31.

37. Xenophon, *Oeconomicus,* in *Conversations of Socrates,* p. 311.

38. In about 399 B.C., the Athenians exiled Xenophon, who was then about thirty, in part because of his friendship with the philosopher Socrates, who that year was convicted (unjustly) of corrupting the city's youth and was executed. Xenophon took refuge in Sparta, but many years later, when he was in his sixties, he was allowed to return to his native city.

39. Plutarch, *Life of Lycurgus,* in *Plutarch on Sparta,* p. 24.

40. Blundell, *Women in Ancient Greece,* p. 111.

41. Mark Golden, *Children and Childhood in Classical Athens.* Baltimore: Johns Hopkins University Press, 1990, p. 83.

42. Golden, *Children and Childhood in Classical Athens,* p. 89.

Chapter 4: The Community Roles and Activities of Classical Greek Women

43. Quoted in Lefkowitz and Fant, *Women's Life in Greece and Rome,* p. 221.

44. Quoted in Lefkowitz and Fant, *Women's Life in Greece and Rome,* p. 267.

45. See J. D. Beazley, *Attic Red-Figure Vase-Painters.* Oxford, England: Clarendon, 1963, p. 571.

46. Quoted in Kathleen Freeman, *The Murder of Herodes and Other Trials from the Athenian Law Courts.* New York: W. W. Norton, 1963, p. 221.

47. Quoted in James Davidson, *Courtesans and Fishcakes: The Consuming Passions of Classical Athens.* New York: St. Martin's, 1998, p. 84.

48. For a detailed, up-to-date discussion of the profession of prostitution in ancient Athens, see Davidson, *Courtesans and Fishcakes,* pp. 73–136.

49. Blundell, *Women in Ancient Greece,* p. 148.

50. Cantarella, *Pandora's Daughters,* pp. 49–50.

51. Robert B. Kebric, *Greek People.* Mountainview, CA: Mayfield, 1997, p. 149.

52. The son, also named Pericles, was illegitimate since his parents were not officially married. He was also a noncitizen because shortly before he was born a law (ironically, sponsored by his father) passed stipulating that only a union of two citizens could produce more citizens, and Aspasia was a foreigner, and therefore a noncitizen. Shortly before his death, however, the elder Pericles made an impassioned plea to the Assembly to confer citizenship on the boy and it did so. The younger Pericles went on to become an Athenian general.

53. Plutarch, *Life of Pericles,* in *The Rise and Fall of Athens: Nine Greek Lives by Plutarch,* trans. Ian Scott-Kilvert. New York: Penguin, 1960, pp. 190–91.

54. Xenophon, *Symposium,* in *Conversations of Socrates,* pp. 230–32.

55. Lefkowitz and Fant, *Women's Life in Greece and Rome,* p. 273.

56. The Eteoboutadai claimed to be the descendants of Athens's original royal family (in the dim past when kings ruled the city).

57. Pomeroy, *Goddesses, Whores, Wives, and Slaves,* pp. 75–76.

58. Manolis Andronicos, *Delphi.* Athens: Ekdotike Athenon, 1993, pp. 10–11.

59. Quoted in Blundell, *Women in Ancient Greece,* p. 152.

60. Quoted in Waldo E. Sweet, ed., *Sport and Recreation in Ancient Greece: A Sourcebook with Translations.* New York: Oxford University Press, 1987, p. 91.

61. Pausanias, *Guide to Greece,* vol. 2, trans. Peter Levi. New York: Penguin Books, 1971, p. 245.

Chapter 5: Greek Women in Mythology, Drama, and Philosophy

62. Pomeroy, *Goddesses, Whores, Wives, and Slaves,* p. 111.

63. Quoted in Keuls, *The Reign of the Phallus,* p. 98.

64. Blundell, *Women in Ancient Greece,* pp. 21–22.

65. Sappho, Fragments 78 and 79, in Balmer, *Sappho,* pp. 78–79.

66. Euripides, *Medea,* in *Euripides: Medea and Other Plays,* trans. Philip Vellacott. New York: Penguin Books, 1963, p. 42.

67. Euripides, *Hippolytus,* in *Three Great Plays of Euripides,* trans. Rex Warner. New York: New American Library, 1958, pp. 99–100.

68. Euripides, *Medea,* in Vellacott translation, pp. 24–25.

69. Pomeroy, *Goddesses, Whores, Wives, and Slaves,* pp. 107–10.

70. Plato, *Republic,* in *Great Books of the Western World,* vol. 7, trans. Benjamin Jowett. Chicago: Encyclopaedia Britannica, 1952, pp. 357–59.

71. Michael Grant, *A Social History of Greece and Rome.* New York: Scribner's, 1992, p. 18.

72. Aristotle, *Politics,* quoted in Lefkowitz and Fant, *Women's Life in Greece and Rome,* pp. 38–39.

Chapter 6: The Lives of Greek Women Improve in the Hellenistic Age

73. Michael Grant, *From Alexander to Cleopatra: The Hellenistic World.* New York: Scribner's, 1982, p. xiii.

74. Pomeroy, *Goddesses, Whores, Wives, and Slaves,* p. 126.

75. Also, the degree of change for women overall may not have been as great as it

appears. Because most of the surviving evidence for the Classic Age comes from Athens, there is the chance that Greek women in areas outside of Athens enjoyed more freedom and opportunities before Hellenistic times than our meager evidence for these places reveals. If so, the changes seen in the Hellenistic Age were less revolutionary and part of an ongoing evolution that began earlier.

76. Grant, A *Social History of Greece and Rome,* p. 22.

77. Grant, *From Alexander to Cleopatra,* p. 195.

78. Quoted in Pomeroy, *Goddesses, Whores, Wives, and Slaves,* pp. 127–28.

79. Quoted in Lefkowitz and Fant, *Women's Life in Greece and Rome,* pp. 14–15.

80. Apollonius of Rhodes, *Argonautica,* trans. E. V. Rieu. New York: Penguin Books, 1971, p. 136.

81. Diogenes Laertius, *Lives of Eminent Philsosophers,* 2 vols., trans. R. D. Hicks. Cambridge, MA: Harvard University Press, 1995, vol. 2, pp. 99–101.

For Further Reading

Denise Dersin, *Greece: Temples, Tombs, and Treasures*. Alexandria, VA: Time-Life Books, 1994. A noteworthy volume that features numerous attractive, appropriate photos and also a long, up-to-date, and beautifully illustrated chapter on Athens's fifth-century B.C. golden age.

Vicki Leon, *Uppity Women of Ancient Times*. Berkeley, CA: Conari, 1995; and *Uppity Women of Medieval Times*. Berkeley, CA: Conari, 1997. Two highly entertaining books that tell the stories of famous women and their struggles during ancient times and on into the Middle Ages. Highly recommended.

Don Nardo, *Cleopatra*. San Diego: Lucent Books, 1994. Covers the life and loves of the famous Greek queen of Egypt in considerable detail and also includes an informative chapter about later literary, artistic, musical, and motion picture depictions of her, including the noted film in which she was portrayed by Elizabeth Taylor.

———, *Greek and Roman Mythology*. San Diego: Lucent Books, 1998. Contains many of the best-known Greek myths featuring female characters, including various goddesses, queens, sorceresses, maidens, and lovers.

———, *Life in Ancient Athens*. San Diego: Lucent Books, 2000. A very useful introduction to ancient Athenian political, social, and religious institutions and practices, with ample descriptions of and citations from the surviving primary sources.

———, *Women Leaders of Nations*. San Diego: Lucent Books, 1999. This entertaining and informative book presents short, readable biographies of notable historical women, including Egypt's Cleopatra; Spain's Isabella I; England's Elizabeth I, Queen Victoria, and Prime Minister Margaret Thatcher; Russia's Catherine the Great; Israel's Golda Meir; and Pakistan's Benazir Bhutto.

Susan Peach and Anne Millard, *The Greeks*. London: Usborne, 1990. A general overview of the history, culture, myths, and everyday life of ancient Greece, presented in a format suitable to young, basic readers (although the many fine, accurate color illustrations make the book appealing to anyone interested in ancient Greece).

Jonathon Rutland, *See Inside an Ancient Greek Town*. New York: Barnes and Noble, 1995. Like Peach and Millard's book, this introduction to ancient Greek life is aimed at grade-school readers; but also like that book, this one is colorful enough to attract some older readers as well.

Major Works Consulted

Ancient Sources in Translation

Author's Note: The most comprehensive single-volume collection of ancient sources about Greek women available is Mary R. Lefkowitz and Maureen B. Fant, eds., *Women's Life in Greece and Rome: A Source Book in Translation.* Baltimore: Johns Hopkins University Press, 1992. The editors, both noted experts on classical women, provide a wide range of material, from the surviving poetry of Sappho, Corinna, and other early poetesses to the writings of Plato and other male philosophers on women's roles and duties. Highly recommended.

Apollonius of Rhodes, *Argonautica.* Trans. E. V. Rieu. New York: Penguin Books, 1971.

Aristophanes, *The Complete Plays of Aristophanes.* Trans. Moses Hadas. New York: Bantam Books, 1962.

Aristotle, *The Philosophy of Aristotle.* Ed. Renford Bambrough. New York: New American Library, 1963.

Josephine Balmer, trans., *Sappho: Poems and Fragments.* Secaucus, NJ: Meadowland Books, 1984.

Diogenes Laertius, *Lives of Eminent Philsosophers.* 2 vols. Trans. R. D. Hicks. Cambridge, MA: Harvard University Press, 1995.

Euripides, *Hippolytus,* in *Three Great Plays of Euripides.* Trans. Rex Warner. New York: New American Library, 1958.

———, *Medea,* in *Euripides: Medea and Other Plays.* Trans. Philip Vellacott. New York: Penguin Books, 1963.

Kathleen Freeman, *The Murder of Herodes and Other Trials from the Athenian Law Courts.* New York: W. W. Norton, 1963.

Hesiod, *Theogony* and *Works and Days,* in *Hesiod and Theognis.* Trans. Dorothea Wender. New York: Penguin Books, 1973.

Homer, *Iliad.* Trans. Robert Fagles. New York: Penguin Books, 1990.

———, *Odyssey.* Trans. E. V. Rieu. Baltimore: Penguin Books, 1961.

Bernard M. W. Knox, ed., *The Norton Book of Classical Literature.* New York: W. W. Norton, 1993. A collection of excerpts from Greek and Roman poetry, drama, and historical writing.

Cornelius Nepos, *The Book of the Great Generals of Foreign Nations.* Trans. John Rolfe. Cambridge, MA: Harvard University Press, 1960.

Pausanias, *Guide to Greece.* 2 vols. Trans. Peter Levi. New York: Penguin Books, 1971.

Plato, *Republic* (and other dialogues), in *Great Books of the Western World.* Vol. 7. Trans. Benjamin Jowett. Chicago: Encyclopaedia Britannica, 1952.

Plutarch, *Parallel Lives*, excerpted in *The Rise and Fall of Athens: Nine Greek Lives by Plutarch*. Trans. Ian Scott-Kilvert. New York: Penguin, 1960.

———, *Parallel Lives, Moralia (Moral Essays)*, and *Sayings of Spartan Women*, excerpted in *Plutarch on Sparta*. Trans. Richard J. A. Talbert. New York: Penguin Books, 1988.

Waldo E. Sweet, ed., *Sport and Recreation in Ancient Greece: A Sourcebook with Translations*. New York: Oxford University Press, 1987. A collection of translations of ancient sources describing sports, games, music, dance, theater, and related leisure activities, accompanied by detailed expert commentary.

Xenophon, *Oeconomicus* and *Symposium*, in *Xenophon: Conversations of Socrates*. Trans. Hugh Tredennick and Robin Waterfield. New York: Penguin Books, 1990.

Modern Sources

Sue Blundell, *Women in Ancient Greece*. Cambridge, MA: Harvard University Press, 1995. One of the best general works on ancient Greek women presently available, this well-informed and well-written book covers all aspects of women's lives (except in the Hellenistic Age, for which see Pomeroy's works below) and consistently provides thorough documentation in quotations from and commentaries on the ancient sources. Very highly recommended.

Eva Cantarella, *Pandora's Daughters: The Role and Status of Women in Greek and Roman Antiquity*. Trans. Maureen B. Fant. Baltimore: Johns Hopkins University Press, 1987. A commendable general introduction to ancient Greek and Roman women, with separate chapters on women in literature and in the writings of the philosophers.

Mark Golden, *Children and Childhood in Classical Athens*. Baltimore: Johns Hopkins University Press, 1990. This detailed, authoritative, and well-documented study of the lives of ancient Athenian girls and boys will appeal mainly to scholars and serious students of ancient Greece.

Michael Grant, *A Social History of Greece and Rome*. New York: Scribner's, 1992. One of many volumes about ancient Greece by this prolific and thoughtful scholar, this clearly written general study is broken down into chapters on specific social groups, including women, freedwomen, slaves, the rich, the poor, and so on.

Richard Hawley and Barbara Levick, eds., *Women in Antiquity: New Assessments*. New York: Routledge, 1995. This collection of essays by noted scholars examines various issues surrounding the study of ancient Greek and Roman women and how the focuses of that study changed during the course of the twentieth century. Will appeal mainly to scholars.

Sarah B. Pomeroy, *Goddesses, Whores, Wives, and Slaves: Women in Classical Antiquity*. New York: Shocken Books,

1975. The groundbreaking volume that helped launch the serious modern study of ancient Greek women is still an important and enlightening source on the subject and provides an excellent starting point for those interested in in-depth further research.

———, *Women in Hellenistic Egypt: From Alexander to Cleopatra.* New York: Schocken Books, 1989. Another fine volume by Pomeroy, this one focuses exclusively on the Hellenistic period, which she covers more concisely (but admirably) in her 1975 book.

Raphael Sealey, *Women and Law in Classical Greece.* Chapel Hill: University of North Carolina Press, 1990. A noted scholar here delivers an informative examination of some of the most important aspects of Greek women's lives—their legal status, rights, and opportunities.

Additional Works Consulted

Manolis Andronicos, *Delphi*. Athens: Ek-dotike Athenon, 1993.

J. D. Beazley, *Attic Red-Figure Vase-Painters*. Oxford, England: Clarendon, 1963.

F. A. G. Beck, *Greek Education, 450–350 B.C.* London: Methuen, 1964.

James Davidson, *Courtesans and Fishcakes: The Consuming Passions of Classical Athens*. New York: St. Martin's, 1998.

N. R. E. Fisher, *Slavery in Classical Greece*. London: Bristol Classical, 1993.

———, *Social Values in Classical Athens*. London: Dent, 1976.

Frank J. Frost, *Greek Society*. Lexington, MA: D. C. Heath, 1980.

Robert Garland, *The Greek Way of Death*. Ithaca: Cornell University Press, 1985.

———, *The Greek Way of Life*. Ithaca, NY: Cornell University Press, 1990.

Michael Grant, *From Alexander to Cleopatra: The Hellenistic World*. New York: Scribner's, 1982.

A. R. W. Harrison, *The Law of Athens: The Family and Property*. London: Clarendon, 1968.

Robert B. Kebric, *Greek People*. Mountainview, CA: Mayfield, 1997.

Eva C. Keuls, *The Reign of the Phallus: Sexual Politics in Ancient Athens*. New York: Harper and Row, 1985.

W. K. Lacey, *The Family in Classical Greece*. London: Thames and Hudson, 1968.

John D. Mikalson, *Athenian Popular Religion*. Chapel Hill: University of North Carolina Press, 1983.

Mark P. O. Morford and Robert J. Lenardon, *Classical Mythology*. New York: Longman, 1985.

Jennifer Neils, *Goddess and Polis: The Panathenaic Festival in Ancient Athens*. Princeton: Princeton University Press, 1992.

Jennifer Neils, ed., *Worshipping Athena: Panathenaia and Parthenon*. Madison: University of Wisconsin Press, 1996. (*Note:* The author's spelling of the great Athenian festival is an acceptable variant of Panathenaea.)

S. M. Okin, *Women in Western Political Thought*. Princeton, NJ: Princeton University Press, 1979.

David M. Schaps, *The Economic Rights of Women in Ancient Greece*. Edinburgh, Scotland: Edinburgh University Press, 1979.

Erika Simon, *Festivals of Attica: An Archaeological Commentary*. Madison: University of Wisconsin Press, 1983.

Index

Picture Credits

About the Author

Historian Don Nardo has written numerous volumes about the ancient Greek world, including *Life in Ancient Athens, The Parthenon,* and *Greek and Roman Sports.* He is also the editor of literary companions to the works of Homer and Sophocles and the forthcoming *Greenhaven Encyclopedia of Ancient Greece.* He resides with his wife, Christine, in Massachusetts.